Crete

- ◀ mountain
- ● town
- ★ palace
- ■ cave

Palaikastro

Mochlos

Gournia

Cave of Dikte

palace of Mallia

Heraklion

palace of Knossos

Arkhanes

Hagia Triada

palace of Phaistos

Tylissos

Mount Ida ◀
Cave of Ida ■

Rethymnon

Kydonia

palace of Khania

D0454524

Plan of the ruins of the palace of Knossos

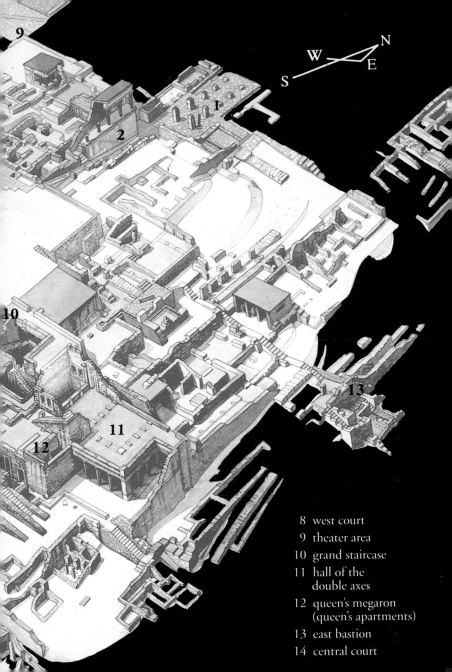

9

N
W   E
S

1

2

10

13

11

12

8 west court

9 theater area

10 grand staircase

11 hall of the
    double axes

12 queen's megaron
    (queen's apartments)

13 east bastion

14 central court

South

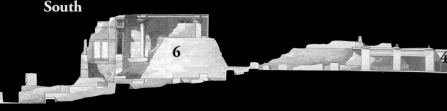

6   4

Longitudinal north–south cross section of the
palace, in its present state, with the south

Above and opposite: Views of the reconstructed palace

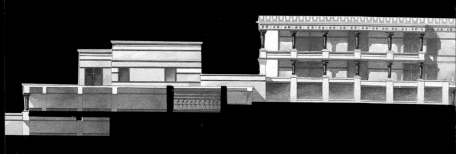

North

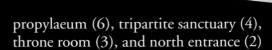

propylaeum (6), tripartite sanctuary (4), throne room (3), and north entrance (2)

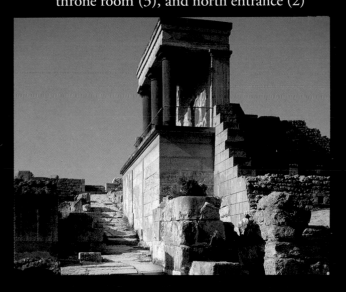

Reconstruction of the same longitudinal north–south cross section of the palace

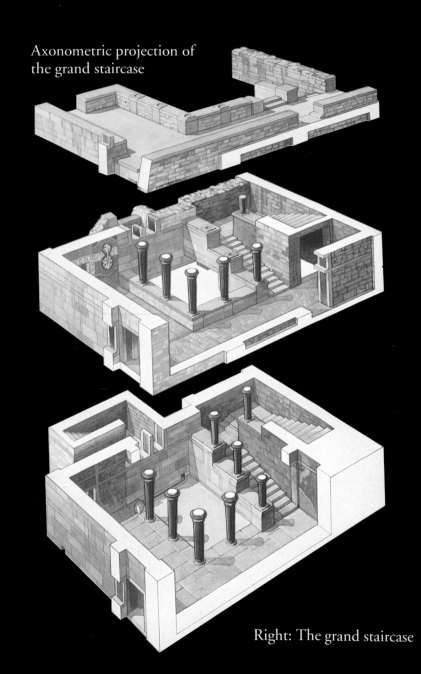

Axonometric projection of
the grand staircase

Right: The grand staircase

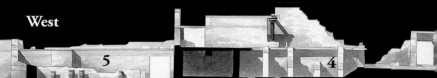

5   4

Longitudinal east–west cross section of the palace, in its present state, with the west storerooms (5), tripartite sanctuary (4), grand staircase (10), and hall of the double axes (11)

Left: The south propylaeum; opposite: The north entrance

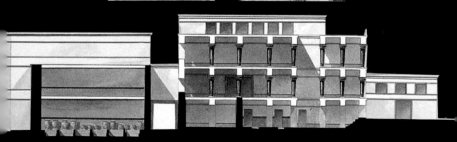

Reconstruction of the same longitudinal east–west cross section of the palace

CONTENTS

KNOSSOS
SEARCHING FOR THE LEGENDARY PALACE OF KING MINOS

Alexandre Farnoux

DISCOVERIES

HARRY N. ABRAMS, INC., PUBLISHERS

"Why, when our history books paint the panorama of the diverse fortunes of the Greek people and the different forms assumed in turn by its genius, why does Crete appear only as a memory?"

Georges Perrot
L'Ile de Crète (The Island of Crete), 1867

CHAPTER I
TERRA INCOGNITA

By the dawn of the nineteenth century, the western powers had forgotten Crete. The attention once given to the island by the Republic of Venice had faded to a dim memory (at left, a view of the Venetian port of Candia on Crete in 1483). Until the period of Venetian occupation there was not even an adequate map of the island (at right, a map by Cristoforo Buondelmonti, 1442).

In the nineteenth century, the Greek island of Crete was relatively unknown to the rest of Europe. In earlier times a few travelers had hazarded a visit: in the fifteenth century the Florentine monk Cristoforo Buondelmonti; in the sixteenth the naturalist Pierre Belon, who was sent to the eastern Mediterranean by King Francis I of France; and in the eighteenth Richard Pococke and Claude Etienne Savary.

Nevertheless, most of the modern world knew the island only from reports in ancient texts. The image of Crete was thus ambiguous: in myth it was the island where Zeus was born, the home of the Bull from the Sea against which the heroes Herakles and Theseus had battled; in history it was the ancient cradle of law

and art, as well as of pirates and liars; land of justice and of triumphant, violent force. This duality is reflected in the mythical figure of Minos, lord of Crete, son of the god Zeus and the mortal Europa: a fickle, cruel king and powerful ruler of the sea who periodically forced the Athenians to sacrifice seven young men and seven young women to the frightful Minotaur imprisoned in his Labyrinth; and yet also a wise king, a lawgiver who received his laws directly from Zeus; because of his spirit of equity, Minos was one of the judges of Hades, the Underworld.

As for the Cretan populace, the consensus of antiquity was unambiguous. Consider the judgment by the sixth-century BC Cretan poet Epimenides: They are, he said, "eternal liars, filthy beasts, lazy bellies!"

An unappreciated voyage

This reputation, which clung to the island for centuries, may explain the slim appeal Crete exercised, despite its beauty, on the wealthy Europeans who

Even in antiquity Crete was a land of ancient legend, as we see in this detail from a fifth-century BC painted cup, in which the Athenian hero Theseus fights the Minotaur, symbol of the injustice and cruelty of the rule of force. The Labyrinth is represented by the mazelike patterns of the wall at right.

Renaissance travelers made maps of Crete's coasts and ports, but rarely went into the interior of the island. Below right: The Bay of Zakro; center: The coast at Messara; left: The plateau of Lasithion.

visited continental Greece in the early nineteenth century, as it struggled for independence from the Turkish Ottoman empire. For them the island was often just a stepping stone on the route from Athens to the Orient; thus the French poet Alphonse de Lamartine wrote in his *Voyage en Orient* (published in English as *A Pilgrimage to the Holy Land*): "Here are the distant mountain peaks of the island of Crete, rising on our right; here is Mount Ida covered with snow looking from here like the lofty sails of a ship upon the sea." Yet a few travelers did stay: the German botanist F. W. Sieber in 1817; the English writer Robert Pashley of Trinity College, Cambridge, in 1834; the Frenchmen Georges Perrot and Léon Thernon of the French School of Athens in 1857; the English poet and painter Edward

The Labyrinth in which the Minotaur was confined was long believed to have been located in a quarry near Gortyna, sketched here by the English writer Edward Lear. Popular traditions about the Labyrinth were a blend of eastern legends and Greek myths. Local belief was that at the heart of the lost Labyrinth was a door with an inscription on it. To anyone able to find and read it, the door would open upon immense treasures.

Lear and the British captain (later admiral) Thomas A. B. Spratt in 1864—to cite only the most famous. What impression did their visits leave on them? The island at that time possessed no known remarkable ruins, such as were to be found on the mainland; the best were at Gortyna from the Roman era and Candia from the period of the Venetian occupation in the Renaissance (the town later became Megalo Kastro, then Heraklion, following Cretan independence). Travelers nevertheless collected coins, fragments of statuary, and inscriptions and identified the scanty sites and ruins as the splendid places mentioned in the texts of ancient historians and geographers. They recorded ancient

Coins collected by travelers to Crete often illustrate famous legends of the island. This one (copied in an engraving by Robert Pashley), minted in the ancient city of Knossos, depicts the Minotaur on the obverse and the Labyrinth on the reverse.

legends, kept alive by popular beliefs, that referred to mythic buildings such as the Labyrinth in which the Minotaur was imprisoned and the tomb of Zeus on Mount Juktas.

Educated visitors were interested primarily in the classical antiquities of Greece and Rome, and were frequently disappointed. Perrot, who visited the site of Knossos in 1857, lamented: "Knossos, the oldest city of ancient Crete, the one that ruled without rival, supreme over all the others, has left no ruins. On the southeastern heights above the small plain where Candia stands is one miserable village whose name, Makrytichos, or the Long Wall, informs the antiquarian that there were once great constructions here; but at most he can detect only the vague, formless debris of mounds of brick."

On the route to the east

However, the island did offer natural wonders: numerous deep grottos, inaccessible mountain peaks, distinctive flora and fauna, such as the local evergreen plane trees and the wild Cretan goats. In 1845 these features attracted the interest of the Muséum National d'Histoire Naturelle in Paris, which sent out an expedition under Professor Victor Raulin of the faculty of sciences at Bordeaux, author of *Description Physique de l'Ile de Crète* (A Physical Description of the Island of Crete).

Picturesque sights were another attraction of an island on the route to Turkey and North Africa: villages where Muslims and Orthodox Christians mixed freely, Cretans

A bove left: Local artisanship and customs fascinated some travelers, who made drawings of scenes of daily life, such as this one by Thomas Spratt of sponge divers in eastern Crete.

dressed in traditional costumes and occupied in traditional crafts—all this fascinated foreigners. Pashley collected popular songs and seasoned his travel writings with them. Cretan Ottoman society thus offered a first touch of exoticism for travelers sailing east from Europe or America, a foretaste of the Orient: "Seeing these low white houses, almost without windows," Perrot wrote, "these flat roofs covered with dried branches, these Muslim women, Arab or Nubian, seated without veils on their doorsteps, while others return from the well bearing on their heads great jugs of red clay, which they support with both arms in a pose that seems borrowed from some fine bronze statue, one could almost be on the shore of the Egyptian Delta, somewhere near Damietta or Alexandria."

In the nineteenth century the town known as Megalo Kastro (Rhabdh-el-Khandak in Arabic, Chandax to the Byzantines, Candia to the Venetians, and Heraklion today) showed many traces of its successive foreign conquerors. Here we see a kiosk-shaped Turkish fountain in Kornarou Square and, to its right, the sixteenth-century Venetian Bembo Fountain, both made from ancient fragments.

A land of contrasts

But this "Orient" was deceptive: The Cretans were by
tradition Orthodox Christians and though they had
converted to Islam they understood neither Turkish nor
Arabic, drank alcohol, and sometimes were secretly
baptized. Even at the turn of the century a visitor could
still write: "This country promises a great diversity of
sights: The palace of Minos and the Venetian battlements,
Christianity side by side with Islam, the Phoenician
question and the Oriental question, art, religion, politics,
history, all mixed together and casting the mind into one
confused revery after another." The people of Crete,
downtrodden and poverty-stricken, quickly won the
sympathy and compassion of foreigners, who were
prompt to denounce their Turkish rulers as exploitive.

Travel in Crete remained a hazardous venture
throughout most of the nineteenth century: Malaria
was endemic in some areas and the roads were badly
maintained and far from safe. The Ottoman rulers were
authoritarian, while the Cretan populace was bitterly
resentful, resistant, and poorly educated. As late as 1907
it took eleven and one-half hours on horseback to go
from Heraklion to Phaistos—a distance of about thirty
miles (fifty kilometers) as the crow flies.

An island in ferment

Western travelers were further discouraged by the
instability of Crete's local politics in the nineteenth
century. Whereas mainland Greece had
been independent since 1830, Crete
long remained part of the Ottoman
empire, despite repeated insurrections
between 1821 and 1898, the year the
island at last won autonomy. In 1867 a
Cretan rebellion against the Sublime
Porte led to bloody reprisals, inspiring
the influential French writer Victor
Hugo, in an appeal published in
the Belgian newspaper
L'Orient, to exclaim:
"Why has Crete risen
up? Because God had

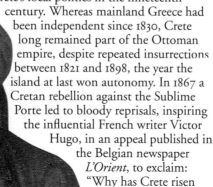

During the Cretan insurrection of 1866–68 the monastery of Arkadi in western Crete was a meeting place for revolutionaries in the independence movement and a refuge for local residents. In November 1866 it was the scene of the bloodiest episode in the rebellion. The Ottoman army attacked, killing many civilians. Three hundred *palikares*, Cretan freedom fighters, fought a desperate battle of resistance, led by the local leader Gabriel; with cries of "Long live freedom!" they blew up the building in which they had barricaded themselves rather than surrender. Below: Paintings of Cretan fighters and their arms.

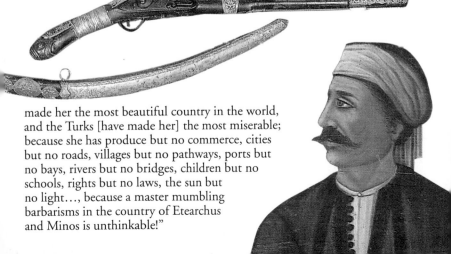

made her the most beautiful country in the world, and the Turks [have made her] the most miserable; because she has produce but no commerce, cities but no roads, villages but no pathways, ports but no bays, rivers but no bridges, children but no schools, rights but no laws, the sun but no light…, because a master mumbling barbarisms in the country of Etearchus and Minos is unthinkable!"

Costume de Crète

N° 170. Edit. Behaeddin Photogr. Candie - C

"Just as the name Minos stands for the political prestige of Crete in earliest antiquity, so Daedalus symbolizes the role of this land in the history of art. Crete arose (during the period of the *Odyssey*) as the commercial and intellectual center of the Greek world, as well as the center of the legends and religious ideas that found expression in the early art of Greece."

Arthur Milchhoefer
Die Anfaenge der Kunst in Griechenland
(The Origins of Art in Greece), 1883

CHAPTER II
IMPATIENCE

Opposite: At the end of the nineteenth century politicians and scholars alike had their eye on Crete: the great powers eagerly followed the exploits of the *palikares*, freedom fighters like the man pictured here, c. 1920, while archaeologists were feverishly seeking traces of King Minos. Right: A sketch of a Minoan seal.

Political unrest did not prevent archaeologists from taking an interest in the island during the last third of the nineteenth century. In fact, they could not help being intrigued by the contrast between ancient texts that described Crete as a pinnacle of Greek civilization and modern travel accounts that stressed the poverty of the few known ruins and the need for thorough

Discovered in 1884, the famous Code of Gortyna (below) is one of the longest Greek inscriptions preserved to date. It contains the oldest law code in Europe, and deals with property rights, slavery, trial procedures, and punishments for crimes. Dating to the early fifth century BC, it is nearly a thousand years later than the Minoan ruins of Knossos.

excavations. Moreover, certain isolated discoveries suggested that the island's past was even more complex than that of the mainland. When Thomas A. B. Spratt came to Palaikastro at the far eastern end of the island, the inhabitants of Angathia, the neighboring village, showed him a tomb that had been opened not long before: "I saw the fragments [of a sarcophagus] that had been recently opened, which was formed of large and thick slabs of terra cotta, rudely ornamented; and some other fragments visible seem to indicate that, in this city, entire coffins or sarcophagi were formed of this material. A very curious terra-cotta figure was obtained

The Cretan cave of Ida, the birthplace of Zeus according to some legends, inspired a cult beginning in the Minoan era. Explored in 1885, the cave was found to contain offerings from many periods: figurines, vases, coins, and inscriptions, including this bronze shield, which apparently depicts the infant Zeus protected by the Curetes, semi-divine beings whose loud dancing and singing, so the tale goes, hid the baby's crying and saved him from his father, Kronos, who desired to kill him. The piece, clearly of eastern origin, encouraged archaeologists' belief that the island had been heavily influenced by the Phoenicians.

from one by a lay priest on a neighboring farm; it seems to be of Phoenician origin, and to indicate a Phoenician settlement or a place of call in their trading-voyages between the eastern and western worlds." This was one of the first references to pre-Hellenic antiquities discovered in Crete.

Archaeologists at work

By 1880 more and more archaeologists were exploring the island, either privately or sponsored by institutions. In the second half of the nineteenth century, several western nations had created archaeological research institutes based at Athens: the French School was founded in 1846, the American School in 1882, the British School in 1885, and the Italian Mission in 1898. Like mainland Greece, Crete became a coveted area for prospecting, and scholars of the various schools wanted to waste no time in acquiring exploration rights to the most promising sites. Among these were Italians (Federico Halbherr, A. Taramelli, Lucio Mariani), Frenchmen (Bernard Haussoulier, André Joubin, P. Demargne), Englishmen (J. L. Myres and Arthur Evans), Germans (Ernst Fabricius, Heinrich Schliemann), and, of course, Cretans, including Minos Kalokairinos and Joseph Hazzidakis. The latter, a physician and intellectual, organized a learned society, the Cretan Syllogos at Heraklion, which became the basis for the city's now-famous archaeological museum. These scholars traversed the island in every direction, surveyed, drew, photographed, made notes, and collected antiquities. Their zeal contrasts sharply with the unenthusiastic accounts of earlier visitors; Georges Perrot exclaimed: "The traveler

Lucio Mariani (seen here in Cretan costume) was one of the pioneer archaeologists who systematically explored Crete, both on foot and by mule. In 1895 he published a long, learned account of the ancient cities he had located, with help from peasants and the writings of ancient geographers.

who explores the coasts of the island and wanders into its valleys will find, on every side, remains of ports, of cisterns dug deep into the rock or constructed at great expense with an indestructible cement, of aqueducts cut from live stone and running up the sides of mountains or cutting right through them to bring water to the cities from far-away springs; he will discover vast quarries like those known by the name 'the Labyrinth of Crete,' which yielded up all the materials for the buildings of powerful Gortyna; from every side, then, the traveler beholds the diverse monuments of industrious wealth, armed with all the arts known to ancient Greece and ruling over an enslaved people." In 1894, in their *History of Art in Primitive Greece*, Perrot and Charles Chipiez extolled the inexhaustible glories of Crete and expressed their impatience to begin excavations. They were agreeing with the Italian archaeologist Paolo Orsi, who lamented in 1890 that Crete, "so renowned in antiquity, has become an unknown land to archaeologists today."

At the dawn of the twentieth century, Crete thus stood as a kind of archaeological El Dorado. What can account for this fascination, this impatience, inspired by an island so long neglected and abandoned?

The first Minoan objects discovered in the nineteenth century were not identified as such. The European museums that acquired bronze figurines from Crete classified them as of doubtful origin (below, the so-called *Dancer* from the Berlin Museum), giving them such labels as "Herakles figures."

Homer and the hundred cities of Crete

The discoveries made by Heinrich Schliemann at Troy in Ionian Turkey (1870) and at Mycenae in southern Greece (1874) were profoundly exciting to the scholarly world and radically changed the attitudes of archaeologists and historians. The excavations sparked a wave of excitement through Europe and America. The treasures found at Mycenae revolutionized existing knowledge of antiquity by revealing the existence, before the era of written records, of a richly developed prehistoric civilization that could be identified with the world of Homer, previously thought to be entirely imaginary. But if the legends were verified at Troy and Mycenae, as Schliemann had brilliantly demonstrated, why was no one able to verify them in Crete? Homer, after all, had said, "There is a land called Crete in the middle of the wine-blue water, a handsome country and fertile, seagirt, and there are many peoples in it, innumerable; there are ninety cities. Language with language mix there together. There are

The excavation of the acropolis at Mycenae in 1874 had a dramatic impact in Europe. Within the ring of tombs inside the city wall was found an unexpected cache of splendid gold objects, left there as funeral offerings. This confirmed the Homeric epithet "Mycenae rich in gold" and conferred a certain historicity on the heroes of the *Iliad* and the *Odyssey*. Schliemann called the funeral mask at left, discovered in Tomb V of circle A, a portrait of Agamemnon, legendary king of Mycenae. No one today still identifies the Mycenaean world literally with that of Homer— the dates are not close enough. Schliemann's rather romantic error was nevertheless fruitful in stimulating interest in Aegean protohistory.

Achaians, there are great-hearted Eteokretans, there are Kydonians, and Dorians in three divisions, and noble Pelasgians; and there is Knossos, the great city, the place where Minos was king for nine-year periods, and conversed with great Zeus."

The high artistic quality of the objects found at Mycenae, such as this damascened dagger (left) from Tomb IV and this gold plaque (below) depicting a sanctuary

Archaeologists believed they had found in Crete the ninety cities of which Homer spoke in the *Odyssey*. As early as 1857 a member of the French School of Athens, Léon Thernon, had delivered to the Académie des Inscriptions et Belles-Lettres a paper titled *Les Cent Villes de Crète* (The Hundred Cities of Crete), based on a survey carried out during two lengthy stays on the island. Schliemann's discoveries had raised the question of the origins of Mycenaean civilization: some thought its source was Phoenicia or Egypt; others imagined an influence from northern Europe; some looked to the Aegean, and to Crete in particular. The attention of specialists now turned to the island of Zeus.

decorated with double horns and birds, amazed scholars, who had long believed that there was no excellent art in Greece or the Aegean before the classical period.

Knossos as a second Mycenae

This keen interest focused, understandably, on finding and excavating the fabled city of Knossos, which Homer had called the capital of the island. A site near Heraklion, known as Kefala hill, had long been identified as its probable location, and this place

The French researcher André Joubin (seen here in an Ottoman army camp) explored Crete on behalf of the French School of Athens, seeking a site to excavate. After the failed negotiations at Knossos, he went to work at the Archaeological Museum of Istanbul, burning his bridges as far as Crete was concerned.

now became the setting for a bitter diplomatic and political battle among scholars.

In 1878, soon after Schliemann's discovery of Mycenae, Knossos was first excavated by Minos Kalokairinos, a Cretan businessman and consul to Spain—a man predestined for the task, one would say, by his first name. He discovered great vases, or *pithoi*, and major architectural remains. His finds were made known to the world in 1881. But he was unable to pursue his work, owing to Cretan hostility to conducting any excavations while the island was still under Ottoman occupation. The island's patriots feared that antiquities might be carted off to Istanbul by the enemy army. Photiades Pasha, Turkish governor of Crete, opposed an 1881 request by the American government to conduct an excavation, as presented by Consul William J. Stillman, on the pretext that Stillman had compromised himself politically in the Cretan rebellions of 1866–68.

Schliemann also took an interest in the site, which he visited in 1886 with Wilhelm Dörpfeld, and again alone in 1889. He wrote in a letter at that time: "I would like to complete my research with a major undertaking: to excavate the prehistoric palace of the kings of Knossos in Crete." His ideas were detailed enough for him to venture the following comment on 17 March of the same year: "I am convinced that the excavations could be carried out in one week with one hundred men."

However, absorbed by his work on the mainland and impeded by the ill will of the Turkish authorities and the greed of the owners of the land, he never executed his plans. After his death in 1890 the Italian Federico Halbherr, the Frenchman André Joubin, and the Englishman Arthur John Evans all attempted to secure the concession for

Minos Kalokairinos wanted to interest foreign archaeologists in the excavation of Knossos, no doubt to ensure that no discoveries would be exported to Istanbul by the Turks. He therefore sent European museums some examples of *pithoi* discovered in his early Knossos excavations (above, the *pithos* offered to the Louvre).

From 1885 to 1914 archaeologists from most of the countries of Europe worked on the island. Seen here (left to right) are Evans, Savignoni, Hazzidakis, Mariani, and Halbherr.

the excavation. Joubin, who made two trips to Crete in 1891, negotiated the purchase of some of the land at Kefala hill with the assistance of the director of the French School of Athens, Théophile Homolle, who stated in a letter written that year: "Crete, in my opinion, is one of the countries that contain the most astonishing ruins, the most crucial discoveries for archaeology; it is essential to gain a foothold there, particularly in the region of Knossos, before the Germans move in."

France seemed well placed to acquire the site. But Evans began negotiating independently in 1894, unbeknownst to the French, and finally purchased a good portion of the land in 1899, with the assistance of King George II of Greece, who was closely related to the British royal family and had thrown his personal support behind the English archaeologist. Relations between the French and British schools at Athens naturally deteriorated at this point.

Meanwhile, after numerous disturbances between 1891 and 1896, the final Cretan insurrection broke out in 1897. Consequently, the negotiations concerning Knossos came to a halt. Since Crete has always held a strategic place in the Mediterranean,

The Turkish occupation of Crete lasted from 1669 to 1898. With autonomy, the entire Ottoman administration disappeared. The last Muslim judge on the island is pictured below.

M^eur Evans ! Joseph Hazzidaihis

The arrival of Prince George in Crete in December 1899 was intended by the great powers to settle the Cretan problem, and thus to resolve some of the political problems of the turbulent eastern Mediterranean.

Evans succeeded in purchasing some of the land at Kefala in 1896, but he had to continue negotiations for some time after excavating began there, before he could take possession of the whole site. He had not reckoned on the strong French competition for Knossos, which dated from 1878. French archaeologists, meanwhile, turned their attention to the Greek mainland, where, in 1891, France was granted the exclusive right to explore Delphi and excavate the great sanctuary of Apollo there.

situated on the route to the Orient and Africa, the European powers followed these developments closely. They did not hesitate to impose a political solution favorable to themselves: The island gained its autonomy in 1898 under the control of the European great powers, who installed the so-called "regime of the Admirals." The island was partitioned among the Italians in southern Crete, the British in the central section of the island, the French in the east, and the Russians in the west. The son of the Greek king became high commissioner of the territory, with a mandate of four years. Annexation to Greece did not occur until 1913. The excavations of Knossos were not able to start in earnest until 1900.

In the space of a few years, a plethora of excavations and discoveries took place on Crete. In this feverish quest, involving all the most powerful nations of Europe, Arthur Evans was motivated above all by a personal quest. His was an adventure both scientific and romantic.

CHAPTER III
IN THE LAND
OF THE GRIFFIN

The story of the discovery of Minoan Crete has elements we normally associate with adventure novels: vanished civilizations, history turned into legend, and buried treasure. The painted griffins of the throne room (detail opposite), or the faience figurine (at right) found in a sealed storeroom, are part of an unexpected world rescued from oblivion.

During his travels in northern and central Europe, Evans collected ethnological, archaeological, and historical information and made a collection of ethnographic photographs, of which two are shown here. He interviewed descendants of the great Venetian families who had settled at Ragusa, organized excavations of tumuli (burials), translated Slavic epics into English, copied classical inscriptions, and made excellent drawings of antiquities and art in the regions he toured (below: One of his travel notebooks; opposite: His watercolor sketch of a fresco detail).

An all-terrain expert

In coming to Crete, Arthur Evans was turning a page in his life. Born in England in 1851 to a well-to-do, cultured family, he had not followed a conventional career path. His father, part owner of a paper-pulp mill, was a historian of some renown, a recognized numismatist, and the owner of an important archaeological collection. He had been a member of an 1859 commission appointed in France to evaluate archaeological discoveries. Arthur might have simply followed in his father's footsteps, but he did not take well to university routine and was bored by business. His half-sister said of him that he was a romantic who needed to escape from the present. He traveled widely in Europe, to France, Finland, Lapland,

and central Europe, where he was official correspondent for the *Manchester Guardian* from 1877 to 1882. He collected antique and archaeological objects he had acquired at markets or in excavations improvised in England on his parents' property, where he often bothered his family with the odor of deerskin or the clutter of packing crates. He spent six years in Ragusa (now Dubrovnik, on the Dalmatian coast of Croatia), explored

A crack reporter in central Europe, Evans became an expert on the question of nationalities: He made a map for the Balkan Committee reflecting ethnic, religious, and political boundaries in

MANCHESTER GUARDIAN

HE REVOLT IN THE HERZEGOVINA.

the region that would be known as Yugoslavia from 1931 to 1991.

Bosnia, Herzegovina, and Albania, and became fascinated by the archaeology and ethnology of that part of Europe.

An ardent democrat, he sympathized with the national minorities of Greece and the Balkans who, freed from the Ottoman empire toward the end of the century, were rapidly becoming the playthings of the western powers. In 1878 he published a series of articles from the Balkans in a book in which he attempted to interest British public opinion in the fate of the Slavs. He ardently advocated giving humanitarian aid to populations victimized by the Turks and the Austro-Hungarian empire. To investigate abuses by the Austrians in Croatia he used archaeological research as a cover. He was arrested on 7 March 1882, by the Austrians, charged with espionage, sentenced to death, and then, after two months' detention in the old Venetian jails of Ragusa, was deported.

Back in England in 1884, he obtained the post of curator of the famous Ashmolean Museum at Oxford University, a position he held until 1908. Despite opposition from the board of trustees, he attempted to define the museum's collections in terms of an archaeology independent of art history, based on concrete research on daily life in the ancient world, on ethnology and prehistory, rather than on aesthetic appreciation of the beautiful objects of the classical age. His inaugural

address was an unabashed plea to make of archaeology a rigorous social science, concerned with the study of humanity from its origins to the present. He traveled to mainland Italy, Sicily, Sardinia, Malta, and Greece to collect antiquities, study folklore, and gather a wide range of information. By the age of forty-nine, in 1900, Evans had already written many scholarly

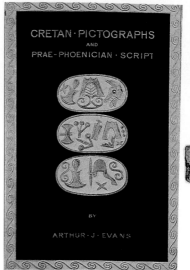

publications, especially on Greek coins from Sicily and the antiquities of Illyria. What was it, then, that drew him to Crete?

The mystery of writing in the age of heroes

Evans closely followed the discoveries made by Schliemann at Troy and Mycenae, visited the 1878 exhibition in London devoted to these finds, and in 1883 met the great German archaeologist in Athens. At the time, researchers were puzzled that a civilization of such obviously high development as that of Mycenae, and that described by Homer hundreds of years later,

had apparently left no written documents. Evans was convinced that some sort of writing system had existed, however primitive, though it was yet to be discovered.

In 1889 he became interested in some small engraved seal stones, sometimes called "stones of the islands," that had been brought to him for the museum's collections; they bore geometric or schematic decorations, some of which he thought might be written characters. According to the antiquarians in Athens from whom Evans made purchases, these stones had come from Crete. He therefore made several visits to the island between 1894 and 1899, collecting numerous stones of this kind. Cretan women wore them on chains around their necks, believing that they helped provide milk for breast-feeding, whence comes their popular Greek name, "milk stones."

During these visits, he noted an abundance of prehistoric ruins, which, following Schliemann's example, he dated to the Mycenaean age. As he grew more convinced that he had found a form of writing, he saw the absolute necessity of starting excavations at

Knossos. He published two articles, in 1894 and 1897, in which he concluded that there had existed not just one form of writing before Homer, but two—one hiero-glyphic (after the manner of Egyptian script) and the other linear, like a modern language. Phoenician writing itself, he believed, was derived from

The treasures of Mycenae soon became known to the public through exhibitions and lectures organized by Heinrich Schliemann in various European capitals (below, the Athens exhibition of 1877). In the nineteenth century, it was assumed that a great civilization must have a form of writing, with historical records and literature. Ancient Egypt and Greece were the exemplars. Jean-François Champollion had deciphered Egypt's hieroglyphics; Evans intended to perform this task for the Homeric world. Despite all his discoveries, he was never to realize this project in full. Opposite: Examples of Minoan seals.

the linear form. This theory implied the existence of a Mediterranean civilization that was neither Egyptian nor Near Eastern, but possibly indigenous to Crete. And this in turn made it all the more urgent that intensive excavations be conducted there, particularly at Knossos.

A dramatic discovery

On 23 March 1900, Evans at last broke ground at the site of Knossos. He spent the next six years there, unearthing the ruins of what turned out to be a great palace, some 43,000 square feet (thirteen thousand square meters) in extension. The site was a complex of many buildings: To the northeast

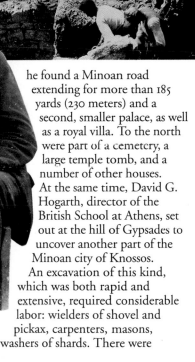

he found a Minoan road extending for more than 185 yards (230 meters) and a second, smaller palace, as well as a royal villa. To the north were part of a cemetery, a large temple tomb, and a number of other houses. At the same time, David G. Hogarth, director of the British School at Athens, set out at the hill of Gypsades to uncover another part of the Minoan city of Knossos.

An excavation of this kind, which was both rapid and extensive, required considerable labor: wielders of shovel and pickax, carpenters, masons, washers of shards. There were

Among the members of the team that gathered around Evans (at left in the photograph), the architect Theodore Fyfe (at center, artist of the fresco copy above) and the ceramics expert Duncan Mackenzie (at right) brought scientific techniques and accuracy to the dig (above, the excavation of the little palace in 1905). Mackenzie was the most familiar with the technical problems of excavation, whereas Evans began with limited experience.

between fifty and three hundred workers on the site during the fifteen to twenty weeks devoted to excavating each year. Evans recruited both Christians and Muslims locally, in the hope that working side by side would foster peaceful relations between the two populations. This was in keeping with his earlier political idealism. In 1903 he had an observation tower built at the western wing of the palace so that he could survey the ever-growing excavation site.

Evans surrounded himself with efficient, reliable colleagues: Duncan Mackenzie supervised the work; a solid Scot, he had dug the site of Phylakopi at Melos. His excavation notebooks remain a model of precision and without him Evans could not have completed his task. Other members of the team were Theodore Fyfe, an architect with the British School at Athens; Christian Doll (starting in 1905), who managed the inventories, plans, and restorations; the Swiss artist Emile Gilliéron (who was later a professor of painting at the court of the king of Greece); and Gilliéron's son Edouard, who made site drawings and worked on fresco restorations.

The archives on these excavations were thorough and, for their time, exemplary. They included the excavation log, kept by Evans and Mackenzie, sketches, inventories, and plentiful photographs. Despite its vast scale, this was one of the first excavations conducted on scientific principles: Evans used stratigraphy (distinguishing each layer of human occupation by its color, texture, or content), preserved evidence as found in certain rooms, examined the contents of vases to determine the nature of the

The Cretan Exploration Fund collected private contributions to finance the British excavations in Crete at the turn of the century.

The Cretan Ex

Patron :

H.R.H. PRINCE GEORGE OF GREECE

High Commissioner of the Powers in Crete.

Directors :

ARTHUR J. EVANS, M.A., F.S.A.,

products they contained, removed delicate discoveries with great care—especially ivory objects—and sifted the earthen rubble in important areas, to search for minute fragments. Most of the finds were removed to Heraklion, though some were left on site. Later this material was also sent to

In 1902 Evans excavated the hall of the double axes in the palace, where he discovered numerous vases and figurines (above). Despite the extent and speed of the

ploration Fund.

the museum at Heraklion, where it remains today. Despite its imperfections, the Knossos dig truly marked a turning point in the history of archaeological excavation in Greece.

The financing of this undertaking was no mean task: Evans received no help from the British or Cretan governments; his funds were entirely private. In 1899 he

dig, the archaeologists—especially Mackenzie—kept precise records in notebooks, such as the one pictured above (inset) of the west house.

launched a subscription in the press, known as the Cretan Exploration Fund; he had better luck with a second appeal in 1907, by which time the project had become famous. The real financing of the excavations at Knossos, however, was through Evans's personal fortune. John Evans, Arthur's father, received endless letters and telegrams from his incorrigible son, announcing the most extraordinary discoveries and regularly begging for more money to continue the search.

His privileged circumstances annoyed more than one person, especially Director Hogarth of the British School at Athens. Without his fortune, Evans could not have conducted the work on such a massive scale, completely independent of all institutions. He himself admitted as much in a letter to his father in November 1900: "The Palace of Knossos was my idea and my work.... I am quite resolved not to have this thing entirely 'pooled' for several reasons, but largely because I must have sole control of what I am personally undertaking.... [M]y way may not be the best, but it is the only way I can work."

"There was a touch of Herculaneum or Pompeii" (Evans)

For the visitor there was nothing remarkable about the site on first viewing. In 1902 Edmond Pottier provided this description: "One's arrival at the excavation site is a surprise. There is no acropolis, no hilltop, nothing at first glance to

suggest a site of such importance. A vast terrain slopes down from the road, beneath bare hillsides marked only by a few wretched shrubs, and descends steeply to the bottom of a ravine with a narrow river; [in this space] are whitened blocks jutting from the earth and workers' silhouettes moving about in a thick cloud of dust. This is the Palace of Knossos."

The first shovelfuls of earth in March 1900 revealed the magnificent throne room, decorated with frescoes of griffins crowned with feathers and with stylized acanthus leaves. The room was so called because it in fact contained a throne, and Evans could not decide if it was meant to seat a king or a queen—he would dearly have loved to place Minos's daughter Ariadne on it! He finally opted for a king, surmising, on the strength of the masculine character of the regal gold masks found at Mycenae, that Knossos had had a male ruler, with a council of twenty elders, seated on the benches that ran round the sides of the chamber.

During the first days of digging he also found what he had first sought at Crete: hundreds of clay tablets inscribed in a writing that he was later to call Linear B. These were

The theater area, unearthed in 1903 (overleaf), is only one part of the vast palace complex of Knossos.

The so-called *Serpent Goddess*, discovered in 1903 along with other cult objects in a Minoan sanctuary, was found in a hiding place beneath a floor of the palace. It offers important clues to Minoan religious practice, customs, and dress.

Opposite: Evans and Hogarth at Heraklion.

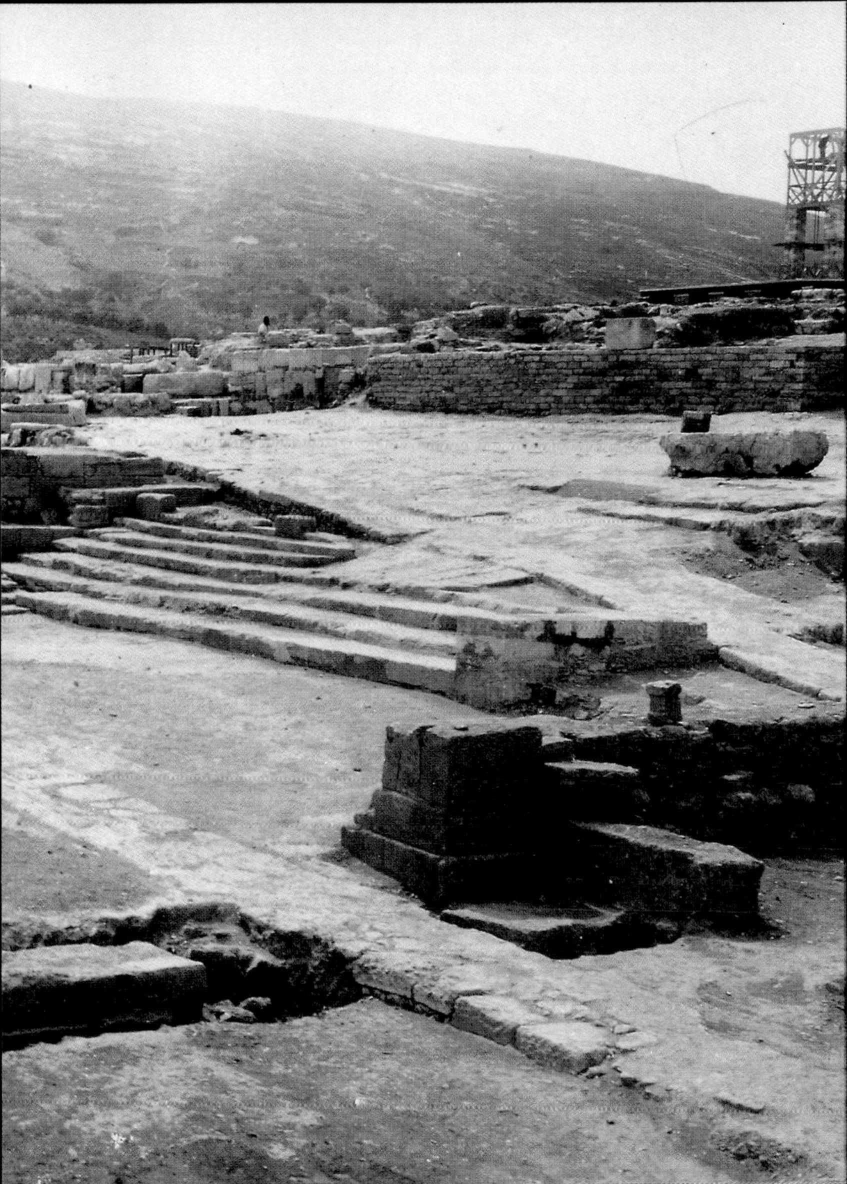

followed by numerous clay documents written in distinct hieroglyphics and in Linear A. Though he could not yet decipher the writing, he believed he had found the archives of the kingdom, a body of laws, correspondence, contracts, trial verdicts, and inventories. In addition, he uncovered the palace's eighteen magazines, or

The west wing of the palace had storerooms off a long corridor that contained large ceramic jars of foodstuffs and agricultural goods, as well as craft objects. Evans found beans in some.

storerooms, some still containing
their storage vases, meant to hold
foodstuffs.

In 1901 Evans carried out the
most spectacular and difficult part
of the palace excavation, the grand
staircase of the east wing, of which

When first discovered in 1901 in the east wing of the palace, the *Bull Leapers* fresco was variously associated with Roman sports and Spanish bullfighting. Its actual meaning remains uncertain.

three successive flights were preserved. Luckily, to manage this work, Evans hired mine workers from Laurion, who spent more than a week digging tunnels that they had to prop up with planks as they proceeded. Another spectacular find of that year was a gaming table of stucco, encrusted with ivory, gold, and crystal (see photograph on page 107). In the same sector, in 1902, he found some faience objects in the form of two-story houses with windows, trees, and animals; these reminded him of the description of Achilles' shield in the *Iliad*. In 1903, in the west wing, he dug up two ditches that yielded a quantity of precious materials—gold, ivory, and crystal, as well as the celebrated *Serpent Goddess* figurine, which he identified as the principal Minoan goddess. He also found many fresco fragments and, each year, hundreds of vases.

Discovery upon discovery was revealed at the dig at Knossos, one of the richest of the century. Evans often compared it to Pompeii. Indeed, the site seemed inexhaustible, and the objects found there were remarkably well preserved. The historic importance of the find impressed the world, as Edmond Pottier noted in the *Revue d'Art Ancien et d'Art Moderne* (Review

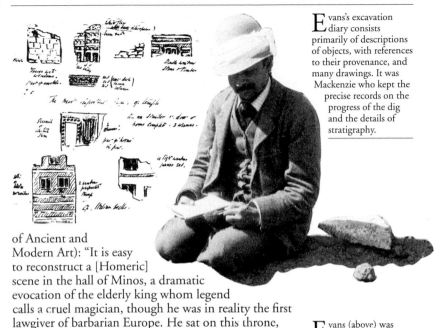

Evans's excavation diary consists primarily of descriptions of objects, with references to their provenance, and many drawings. It was Mackenzie who kept the precise records on the progress of the dig and the details of stratigraphy.

of Ancient and Modern Art): "It is easy to reconstruct a [Homeric] scene in the hall of Minos, a dramatic evocation of the elderly king whom legend calls a cruel magician, though he was in reality the first lawgiver of barbarian Europe. He sat on this throne, placed his feet on this stone, and his voice resonated through the room; [standing] there, one feels fully the moving, poetic realities that archaeology reveals. It took just a few spadefuls of dirt to convert a legend into history, and thus history in turn entered the modern world."

Evans (above) was deeply excited by the discovery of faience plaques depicting house facades (below), which indicated that prehistoric Crete had towns with multistoried houses very close to the modern type.

Crete becomes one vast excavation site

These were not the only discoveries made in Crete at the turn of the century. Beginning in 1900 the Italian team of Halbherr, Luigi Pernier, L. Savignoni, and Roberto Paribeni started to excavate a palace at Phaistos on the south coast and a great villa at nearby Hagia Triada; the Americans Harriet Boyd, Edith H. Hall, and Richard B. Seager were digging in eastern Crete, at Kavousi, Gournia, Vassilike, Pseira, and Mochlos, where they uncovered a whole city and its necropolis; the Englishmen Hogarth, R. M. Dawkins, and R. C. Bosanquet explored the Cave of Psychro, where Zeus is said to have been raised, the sanctuary at the peak of Petsopha, and parts of the cities of Knossos, Palaikastro, and Zakro; the

Tylissos was excavated by Hazzidakis and Xanthondidis (below) between 1902 and 1913. Hazzidakis uncovered three sizable houses there with abundant contents, including terra-cotta and bronze vases.

Cretans Hazzidakis and Stephanos Xanthoudidis were digging the great residences at Tylissos, a villa at Nirou Khani, and tombs at Koumasa and Mouliana. The French, the last to join the fray after their setback at Knossos and a fruitless effort at Goulas (the modern town of Lato), concentrated their efforts on the site of Mallia, which, with Hazzidakis, they began to explore in 1915.

This young American woman, Harriet Boyd, amazed the largely male archaeological establishment when she excavated the site of Gournia in eastern Crete under difficult conditions. Between 1901 and 1904 she uncovered an entire Minoan town.

Most digs in Crete concentrated on prehistoric sites. Only the Italians at Gortyna excavated a site from the classical period, Hellenic and later, and made an initial survey of the Renaissance-era Venetian ruins on the island.

The taste for adventure

Cretan archaeology was teeming with colorful personalities.

Crete offered untold surprises to the first archaeologists, such as Gerola (below) who explored the palm forest of Vai.

Marthe Oulié and Hermine de Saussure, at the end of their stay on the island, described their adventure in these terms: "We were sorry to leave noisy, dusty Candia [Heraklion], whose

There was the Italian Federico Halbherr criss-crossing the island on a horse (either white or black, depending on the legend), or the American Harriet Boyd, who explored the Minoan city of Gournia and later published her findings with two other women, Blanche E. Williams and Edith H. Hall. Two young Frenchwomen, Marthe Oulié and Hermine de Saussure, cruising the Mediterranean and the Greek isles, disembarked at the bay of Mallia out of curiosity. They obtained permission to dig a portion of the Minoan city and won a place in the island's lore as "the young girls of Mallia."

In all the excitement over Cretan archaeology, the island's strategic position was not forgotten by the various national groups working there. The Briton John Pendlebury, for instance, worked with Evans in Crete in 1929 and when the Second World War began was able to give the British army the benefit of his detailed knowledge of the terrain. In so doing, he played a decisive role in the struggle of the Cretan resistance against the Germans in 1941.

facades and minarets faded in the distance amid lofty purplish mountains, misted with sunlight. In two months, interrupted by frequent excursions to the Minoan sites of Messara in the east and the high plains at the island's center, we had uncovered a corner of the pre-Hellenic city of Mallia, spending our days on the site in the torrid sun and nights under a shelter of branches beside the sea."

Italian excavation sites

The site of Hagia Triada was excavated by the Italians from 1902 to 1914. In addition to a remarkable, elaborate architectural complex, furnishings were found there of great richness: finely sculpted steatite vases, a sarcophagus painted with religious scenes, inscribed tablets, fresco fragments, seals, bronze ingots, and terra-cotta figurines. Together with the palace of Phaistos, excavated at the same time, it provided ample documentation of the civilization that had arisen on Cretan soil.

Overleaf. At the turn of the century the Italians started their excavation at Gortyna, at the time the only Hellenic and Roman site known in Crete. Gerola, who took part in this effort (he stands near the church of Saint Titus in 1900), also made a series of remarkable photographs of contemporary Crete and of its Venetian and Turkish monuments.

"The excavations of Mr. Evans are a major event in the history of archaeology; they reveal to us a civilization much richer and more advanced than the one we had learned about from Schliemann's discoveries; they put to rest all the theories that assign the Phoenicians a dominant role in the ancient civilizations of the [Aegean] archipelago."

Salomon Reinach, 1902

CHAPTER IV
THE MAGICIAN OF KNOSSOS

Evans was very much an inventor: He discovered an unknown world and analyzed its history. With the help of images discovered at Knossos and elsewhere in Crete (such as that to the right, on the sarcophagus of Hagia Triada), he was able to bring to life the ruins that archaeologists were uncovering on the island. What he could not find he created; the *Prince with Lilies* fresco (opposite) is largely a speculative invention.

In setting his sights on Knossos, Evans had expected to unearth a Mycenaean palace of the same period and type as those found by Schliemann on the Greek mainland a few decades earlier. He thus hoped to contribute to research on Homeric Crete, which he assumed was the same age as Knossos. "The great days of Crete," he wrote, "were those of which we still find a reflection in the Homeric poems" (*The Academy*, 20 June 1896). In his excavation reports of 1900 and 1901 on the finding of the megaron, the royal apartment of the palace, he described a fortified entryway to the north and compared it with that at Mycenae, again imagining that the sites were coeval. He often turned to Homer to breathe life into the ruins he unearthed, as when he dug the west court: "It takes no great effort of the imagination to picture, in the Mycenaean age, the Council of Elders seated here while the king himself occupies the throne of Justice near the gates to the palace." This notion was widely shared by specialists: Crete was thought at the time to be the center of a culture called "Mycenaea."

A civilization in the fullest sense

But Evans realized soon enough that what he was unearthing did not correspond to what was known of the Mycenaeans: The palace of Knossos, remarkably, was not fortified; among the hundreds of objects with figurative paintings found in the excavations, very few portrayed warriors or soldiers and the great majority of the ceramics differed in many particulars from the types and forms found on the mainland. Little by little Evans came to doubt that the Mycenaeans had inhabited this labyrinthine palace—unless perhaps at a later date. He

Ceramics discovered in Crete, particularly in the Kamares Cave in 1890, presented features quite different from mainland examples (above: A polychrome bowl found at Knossos in 1903). Evans assumed at first that Mycenaean soldiers had invaded the island, discovered a local culture, and assimilated it into their own. Only later did he realize that the Cretan ceramics were earlier than Mycenae. Left: A figure of a Mycenaean soldier wearing a boar's-tooth helmet.

"We are no mere relic-worshippers," Evans stated in 1884. "Our theme is history—the history of the rise and succession of human Arts, Institutions, and Beliefs."

began to perceive that he was dealing with a different civilization entirely. At first he thought that this was a regional variant of Mycenaean civilization, and then decided it must be an indigenous culture—that of the mysterious Eteocretans mentioned by Homer (*Odyssey*, XIX, 176), who had been swiftly

The discovery of Knossos in 1900 gave Evans (below) the opportunity to apply the archaeological methodology that he had urged upon the Ashmolean Museum.

conquered by the Mycenaeans. But in the end, faced
with such an abundance of artworks, objects, and styles
with no known mainland parallels, he concluded that
he had come upon a civilization independent of that of
the Mycenaeans and, above all, older than theirs.

To establish clearly that his discoveries surpassed
Schliemann's in importance, Evans spoke before the XIIIth
International Congress of Prehistoric Anthropology and

Archaeology in 1905, announcing that in his view the
Mycenaean was no more than a belated offshoot of the
Minoan. This marked a major advance in the study
of early antiquity. Since Schliemann's discoveries, the
question of the origin of Mycenaean civilization had been
the subject of much debate. Stepping into the dispute
between those who traced it to northern Europe and those
who insisted on Near Eastern roots, Evans came up with
an unexpected solution: He discovered a new world
nearby, dating to an earlier era than either.

Origins: Between myth and archaeology

Once the originality of this culture, which
Evans dubbed the Minoan, had been
established, it then had to be described.
Schliemann had been able to
draw upon Homer and the
literature of antiquity to
form a picture of Mycenaean
civilization. Evans, however, had
few direct ancient sources on Crete at his

disposal: The Minoan world had left scant traces in human memory, and what existed in the texts was so altered, so fragmentary, so mixed with legend that it was difficult to use and unreliable. A phrase here, a name there was all that could be found in the writings of the Greek culture that followed the downfall of the Minoan.

There were some precedents for postulating a pre-Mycenaean culture on Crete. In 1866 chance had uncovered the ruins of a prehistoric city under the ashes of the volcano on the Aegean island of Thera (modern Santorini), north of Crete. Archaeologists were able to confirm that this had been a very old city, undoubtedly older than the Mycenaean city-states of the mainland, but they could not establish a precise date for it because the artifacts discovered there bore no resemblance to

The volcano on Thera, modern Santorini (opposite bottom: The island in the fifteenth century), remained active from 1500 BC. It erupted dramatically in AD 1866 (above). Excavation of Thera (beginning in 1967) has revealed the best-preserved prehistoric city in Europe; an area of over 33,000 square feet (10,000 square meters) has been uncovered to date (opposite top).

any other known material. Geological evidence provided a date that seemed hardly credible: 2000 BC. Some drew the conclusion that this was some sort of barbarian, prehistoric Pompeii whose existence had never been guessed. Others chose to identify Thera with the Atlantis of legend.

Similarly, from 1896 to 1899 at Phylakopi on the isle of Melos the British excavated the remains of another prehistoric city, which appeared to be contemporary with Thera. Thus, for several years there had been growing a body of evidence for a pre-Mycenaean culture unique to the Mediterranean and independent of the great civilizations of Egypt and Asia. In 1893 the Egyptologist Flinders Petrie announced the discovery of objects made in the Aegean style at the Egyptian site of Kahun, in Fayum. These objects were contemporary with the 12th dynasty of Egypt, thus confirming the great age of Thera and Melos, and indicating that those islands had traded with Egypt. The growing list of discoveries in Crete between 1900 and 1905—especially the simultaneous excavation of the palaces of Knossos and Phaistos—left no further ambiguity: Aegean prehistory was born.

The world of Minos

The first problem faced by Evans was the matter of just what to call this civilization. Should it be *Knossian,* on the model of Schliemann's *Mycenaean,* or perhaps *Creto-Mycenaean*? Evans

The discovery of the Phaistos disk (left) in 1908 suggested that the original culture on Crete was indigenous, not a colony of an outside civilization. The inscription, with its 242 symbols or glyphs stamped in fresh clay, sparked great interest. Almost a century later, the disk remains a riddle, defying all attempts to decipher it.

The rich archaeological material unearthed (opposite, stone pots and vases from the western wing of the palace of Knossos) was evidence of a highly developed culture, quite unexpected for such an early date.

Evans assigned some of the symbols he found to Minoan royalty; at left is the so-called lily crown.

opted for the term *Minoan*, derived from the name of
the first, mythic king of Crete, Minos, founder of a
dynasty of ancient kings. To define and describe Minoan
civilization Evans could turn to the abundant material
discovered during the excavations. But all this bric-a-brac
had to be organized to form a coherent vision of a
culture. Evans assumed this task; he would, in a sense,
invent Minoan civilization.

In addition to the excavations that Evans carried out
until 1935, he published a monumental six-volume
synthesis of his research between 1921 and 1935. Titled
The Palace of Minos at Knossos, it was produced with
astonishing speed. The work deals with myriad topics,
from Minoan chronology to clothing; from architecture
to frescoes, inscriptions, terra-cotta vases, and other art
objects; from earthquakes to agriculture—in each case
with an erudition that is nothing short of remarkable.
Evans not only reports on the material drawn from his

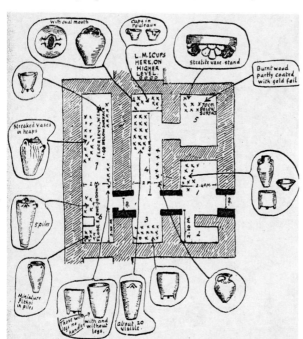

The Palace of Minos
is a unique sort of
scholarly publication.
At first entitled *Nine
Minoan Periods,* this
vast work is a veritable
scientific saga. It was a
publishing feat, too, for
Evans was a difficult
author, rewriting whole
sections during printing
and demanding
numerous complex
illustrations, such as that
at left. Corrections ended
up costing more than
the typesetting.

The illustrations in *The Palace of Minos* were intended not only to provide information on the material discovered, but also to resurrect a vanished civilization. On the basis of data observed during the dig, Evans re-created episodes in court life, such as this fictional view of the king in the hall of the double axes on a winter's evening. These illustrations, plentiful and widely reproduced, played—and continue to play—an important role in modern perceptions of the Minoan world.

excavations, but acknowledges and incorporates the major discoveries—such as the ceremonial arms from Mallia—in the other excavations in Crete. He cites parallel discoveries in Egypt, Malta, and Italy. These volumes, illustrated with innumerable drawings, sketches, watercolors, plans, and photographs, form a veritable encyclopedia of Minoan civilization. The scope of the undertaking is still staggering. It is the work of a pioneer who laid the groundwork for all future Minoan archaeology. In many respects this work has not been surpassed. One flaw in Evans's presentation is that in order to exalt Minoan civilization he attempted to reduce Mycenaean cities to the status of mere colonies, eclipsing a whole sphere of Aegean prehistoric studies, especially the deciphering of archives written in Linear B.

Behind the scenes of an invention: Architectural stratigraphy

Initially, in any case, Cretan writing was indecipherable. In the absence of a written record, Evans's plan to reconstruct the Minoan world had to depend entirely on

The rooms called the queen's private apartments, with a lavatory, bathroom, and a room with alcoves opening on a light shaft, particularly inspired Evans. To bring the ruins to life he had colored illustrations made of the interiors as they might once have been, with furnishings based on some found in the palace. Figures modeled on those of the Minoan frescoes populated these scenes. This type of illustration expresses the rather romantic desire to fill the silences of ancient texts: Evans, in fact, had no direct testimony concerning life in the kingdom of Minos—unlike Schliemann, who drew freely on Homer to evoke the later world of Troy and Mycenae. The charming, if largely invented, iconography seen here was to become very popular. The queen in the novel *L'Atlantide* ("Atlantis") by Pierre Benoit was housed in an apartment based on Evans's models.

the data from the excavation and the objects he and his fellow archaeologists discovered. He was therefore careful to direct the excavation in the modern method, with due awareness of the physical context of each discovery. Thanks to the full-time presence of an architect on the site—quite a novelty at the time—he was able to supplement the observations and summaries entered in his notebooks with precise sketches.

Evans used a technique then called "architectural stratigraphy," of which he was a pioneer. By documenting each layer, or stratum, of earth as he removed it, and recording the depth at which each object, from humble potsherd to gilded statue, was found, he was able to establish a chronology of successive states of the palace, which he named; thus he distinguished the "First Palace period (1800–1700 BC)" and the "Second Palace period (1650–1450 BC)," and concluded that the Mycenaeans had occupied Knossos for only a very brief time, just before the final abandonment of the city. From the

Excavation of the palace of Knossos was a real feat of engineering. Some areas had two or more levels to be preserved and it was also necessary to distinguish between different states or time periods within a single floor. Some dug areas were nearly forty feet (twelve meters) deep. The presence of imported objects (opposite right: A lid bearing the cartouche of the Egyptian King Hyksos Khyan, fifteenth century BC) provided some firm dates.

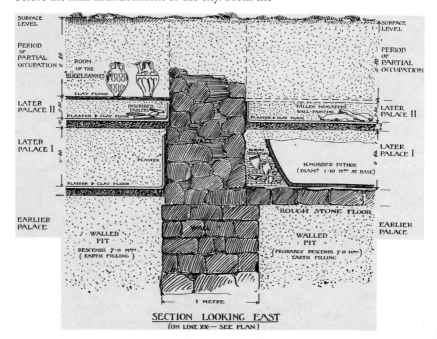

SECTION LOOKING EAST
(ON LINE XX — SEE PLAN)

soundings he had made he established stratigraphies, in which the material from each stratum served to define a stylistic phase. Finally, the discovery of Egyptian objects of identifiable and datable styles found in the palace allowed him to establish a link between the Minoan world and ancient Egypt.

By 1905 he had begun to construct both a relative and an absolute chronology for all of Minoan Crete, divided into three great periods: Early, Middle, and Late Minoan; each of these was broken down further into three subperiods. Like many scientific thinkers of his time, he was strongly influenced by the evolutionary theories of Darwin in the creation of a historical structure. Gustave Glotz noted in 1923 in *The Aegean Civilisation:* "Evans, it is obvious, combines the data from stratification with the universal laws of evolution and the demands of the human spirit." In its main outlines, his Minoan chronology is still in use today.

Describing the past

For the study of artifacts, Evans began by associating the unknown with the known, according to a basic principle of comparative archaeology. He made frequent comparisons among widely varying cultures: Egypt, Syria, the

The aesthetic quality of the Minoan objects (here the Boxers' *rhyton,* or libation cup, from Hagia Triada) caused great excitement among art historians. Adolphe Reinach wrote: "Frescoes recalling the naturalism of Japanese paintings, painted stucco reliefs of unsurpassed realism, hard stones and gems, objects of ivory and steatite chiselled with a fineness unparalleled until the Renaissance, pottery affording patterns to all modern lovers of fired earthenware and rare faience, jewellery of floral design, enriched with enamel as well as with precious stones, such as our own Laliques [jewelers] are only just beginning to make anew: such are the masterpieces with which the Minoans adorned their dwellings for nearly a thousand years."

Etruscans, and the Romans were cited in turn, as well as, more incongruously, Japanese, Renaissance, and medieval art. These comparisons allowed him to describe the features of this new world in approximate and relative terms; for instance, discovering the faience idols in 1903, he wrote: "The Palace manufactory of Knossos is the remote predecessor of Vincennes and Sèvres, of Medicean Florence, of Urbino or Capodimonte, of Meissen, and other princely establishments of the same kind."

Evans sought elements of comparison as far afield as India; he compared the layout of the ruins he uncovered to that of a Roman camp, the elevation to that of an Italian Renaissance palace. Each object found in the excavation suggested to him possible stylistic links to the furnishings of more recent periods; the elegant stone chair that he called the throne of Minos, for instance (and which he had copied in wood for his Oxford home and to give to friends), reminded him of a Gothic prayer stool, with its undulating contour and the ogival ornament under the seat. In the writings of some careless enthusiasts, Minoan art became a composite of the whole history of art. This reliance on comparative techniques is frequent in the writings of all the experts on Minoan civilization up to the 1930s; it betrays their perplexity when faced with a civilization that seemed to have little in common with classical antiquity.

When he first discovered the throne, Evans imagined that it had been intended for a woman rather than a man and called it the throne of Ariadne, the daughter of Minos and Pasiphaë. The width of the seat suggested that it had accommodated full skirts, such as he saw in frescoes and figurines. (Left: A wooden reconstruction of the throne.)

Ethnology meets archaeology

To understand the functions of the objects he found, Evans used the principles of ethnology. He was convinced that certain current practices

Crete at the turn of the twentieth century had retained lively folk traditions, notably in dance and music. Evans drew similarities between the dances performed by his workers and the dance depicted in a set of figurines discovered at Palaikastro (below). These dances could not fail to remind him of Homer, who had said of Knossos: "The renowned smith…made elaborate on it a dancing floor, like that which once in the wide spaces of Knossos Daidalos built…. There were young men…and young girls, sought for their beauty with gifts of oxen, dancing, and holding hands at the wrist. These wore, the maidens long light robes, but the men wore tunics of finespun work…. At whiles on their understanding feet they would run very lightly,…they would form rows, and run, rows crossing each other." (*Iliad*, XVIII, 590 ff.)

of traditional life—in Crete or in central Europe, for instance—could explain some of the ancient customs of which he found traces, particularly in the area of religious beliefs. This methodology of using present customs to speculate about past ones has been largely discredited, but was much in vogue at that time. Evans had been interested in ethnology ever since his travels in Bosnia and Croatia and his discussions on the subject with his father. Thus he did not hesitate to make an association between the so-called cult of the pillar, which he considered one of the fundamental elements of Minoan religion, and a pre-Islamic cult of northern Macedonia into which he had been initiated during one of his journeys. Similarly, he studied

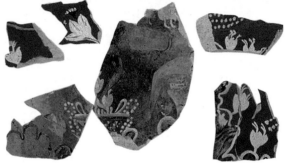

traditional Cretan dances and compared them to Theseus's crane dance, as described in ancient texts, or to a Minoan painting of dancers. He was interested in Cretan pottery makers who still produced *pithoi* identical to those found in the palace storerooms.

A wordless book of images

Evans may not have had reliable ancient texts to draw on, but he did have access to abundant iconography in the paintings and sculptures of Knossos. He proposed the theory that the images of the Knossos frescoes were historical or documentary in nature. Thus he used the art found in the excavations to describe Minoan society and the rites of court life. A decorated sarcophagus discovered at Hagia Triada by the Italians in 1903, as well as depictions of ritual scenes on many stamps and seals, gave him the

Religious themes are perhaps the most frequent elements in Minoan iconography. This seal stamp (below) found at Knossos depicts, from left to right, the facade of a sanctuary and the mother goddess, flanked by lions guarding the sacred mountain, before which a worshiper stands.

The initial restoration of some Minoan frescoes was marred by significant errors: At near left, six fragments found in the northern area of the palace were integrated into a harvesting scene, called the *Saffron Gatherer,* that fit Evans's preconceptions of the Minoan world as a paradise where people lived in harmony with nature. Later studies revealed that the fresco actually depicted a monkey (opposite).

rudiments with which to reconstruct (and partly invent) a Minoan religion whose central figures were a mother goddess—goddess of fertility and mistress of the beasts—and her young masculine associate, of whom Minos was the representative on earth. Evans thus made the Minoan ruler a priest-king, some of whose attributes he borrowed from the pharaohs of ancient Egypt and from the medieval papacy.

He attempted to identify portraits of the king and of a young prince. He believed that Knossos had reigned widely over the Aegean, Melos, and the Mycenaean mainland, thanks to a powerful navy.

Evans had no hesitation, either, about reconstructing missing images, including the famous *Prince with Lilies* fresco, which was mistakenly pieced together from fragments belonging to different frescoes. He even went so far as to transpose into a fresco the depiction found on a seal—a seal whose authenticity was later questioned. In parallel with his publicizing of Minoan images, Evans ordered a great number of graphic reconstructions of the palace, which were widely circulated and served as a

This seal, Evans speculated, contained the portrait of one of the kings of Knossos, followed by his signature.

Discovery

On 13 April 1900, Evans discovered the palace throne room, decorated with griffin frescoes and containing a carved stone seat. From the floor he collected stone vases, bits of fresco, and fragments of gold, crystal, and earthenware. A telegram to *The Times* in London informed the world of the discovery of the throne of Minos. Like Schliemann, who a few decades earlier had telegraphed King George I of Greece that he had just discovered the tombs of the Homeric kings, Evans invited the modern-day king of the Hellenes to "sit on the oldest throne of Europe."

Reconstruction

The throne room was the subject of numerous efforts at protection and interpretation (below: A page from Evans's excavation notebook, 14 April 1900).

The restorer Gilliéron and the architect Fyfe worked on both the graphic reconstruction of the rooms (left: An unfinished watercolor by Gilliéron) and their preservation. The throne room, particularly prestigious, underwent several reconstructions before the one done in 1930 in the antique style.

Imagination

Evans imagined the Minoan kingdom as ruled by a priest-king supported by a council. This reconstruction of the throne room as assembly hall illustrates the theory: At right is the throne, flanked by a bench running along walls painted with griffins and plants; at left, behind a balustrade, is a purificatory bath for ritual ablutions; at the rear is a small sanctuary with cult objects (double horns, double axes, and statuette). The vases found on the floor were, he thought, being used during a ceremony that was abruptly interrupted by the catastrophe that destroyed the palace. In his texts, Evans portrayed the Minoan king as a pious ruler, powerful and peace-loving—the opposite of the petty rulers of Homeric epics, combative men who defied the gods and sometimes practiced piracy. This image of Minos also clashed with ancient sources that described the legendary ruler as despotic and violent.

A miniature fresco from the northern part of the palace (at left) showed some buildings, which Piet de Jong relied on to draw the facade of the western wing of the palace on the central court (below). De Jong was also guided by architects' notes made during the excavation.

model for Piet de Jong in the American excavations at the mainland Greek site of Pylos in 1939. Evans thus imposed, step by step, on the reality he found in the ruins of painted walls and paved floors the image of a flourishing and peaceful civilization that had extended over most of the eastern Mediterranean.

Evans the restorer

The artworks of Knossos made it possible not only to reconstruct

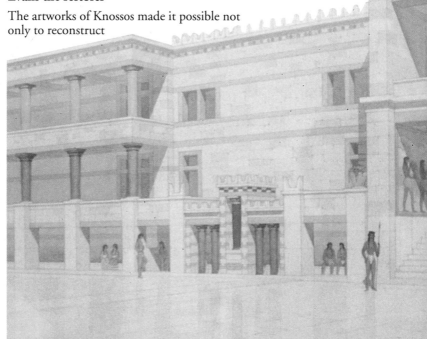

Minoan civilization on paper, but also to undertake restoration and literal reconstruction work on the site. Evans soon realized that he could use architectural elements depicted in certain fresco fragments as an aid to reconstructing the palace itself. In 1902 Fyfe described the principles of restoration of the palace of Minos, and the work got started during the first excavation campaign. Evans worked from renderings, plans, and photographs, inspired by a strong commitment to preserve the ruins. Minoan architecture had been built of earth, wood, and stone. Rain and temperature fluctuations were threats to the newly unearthed palace. In 1905, when Evans

Evans's contemporaries were astonished by the Cretan monuments, especially their vivid, beautifully preserved colors and the originality of the floor plans. Salomon Reinach said of the palace of Knossos: "The general impression of the exterior must have been similar to that of mosques faced in faience, while the inside no doubt resembled that of the richest Pompeian apartments." The tapered form of the columns, as well as their bright red color, caused considerable surprise and inspired some modern architects, such as Jože Plečnik, who restored Prague Castle between 1927 and 1931.

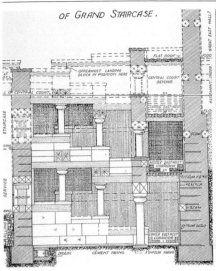

and Mackenzie resumed their work after a hiatus, they found the palace badly damaged by the winter rains, requiring major reinforcement and reconstruction work. It is often forgotten today that some of these restorations were considerable achievements, as was the work on the grand staircase, in danger of collapsing after its excavation. In a *Times* (London) article of 31 October 1905, Evans described how he had dismantled the topmost flight in order to reinforce the lower supports and had used bricks, metal girders, and cement to replace the columns and lintels that had burned in the ancient fire that had destroyed the palace. Controversial though modern materials were, Evans did not hesitate to use concrete; in a lecture to the Society of Antiquaries of London in 1926, he praised its flexibility and strong resistance to seismic disturbances. An earthquake that same year showed that it was in some ways a good choice, although poorly aging reinforced concrete causes a number of conservation problems today.

The architect Christian Doll (at rear) drew plans (left) for reinforcing and reconstructing the grand staircase.

Evans the visionary

Evans's work caused lively debate in the popular press, in which a romantic nostalgia for ruins mingled with disapproval of the whims of a rich British dilettante. René Dussaud voiced this irritation when he wrote in 1907: "The brazenness of Evans' actions drew strong criticism, to the point where it is generally believed that this clever archaeologist is completely rebuilding the palace of Minos from scratch. It would certainly have been preferable if the restoration of certain portions had not gone too far and if the visitor could have been spared the unpleasant impression of entering a completely redecorated apartment. As a result—and this is the most serious point—the task of verification has been made difficult." One French journalist dubbed Evans "the builder of ruins."

Evans admitted, not without irony, that the sight of the reconstructed palace of Knossos was likely to shock lovers of picturesque ruins. It is important to understand the spirit in which he

Evans was very proud of the grand staircase, unique in architectural history. It was, he wrote, more modern in conception than anything else handed down from Greek and Roman antiquity. Its complexity, like that of the overall plan of the palace, persuaded the archaeologist that he had found the Labyrinth of legend. Below: Work on the grand staircase.

approached this work. To preserve the ruins inevitably involved making choices based on probabilities and the subjective interpretation of fragments. This task Evans took most seriously: Three times he altered the temporary covering of the throne room before settling on a reconstruction that satisfied him. He thought he

In less than a decade, the principal work of restoring the palace was complete. It had been financed in large measure by Evans's personal fortune.

had sufficient source material to reconstruct the splendors of the royal residence accurately. In the process, he wanted to give concrete form to his conception of the Minoan world. Nothing tells us more about the overall perspective in which he operated than these lines from his monumental and scrupulous book: "During an attack of fever, having found, for the sake of better air, a temporary lodging in the room below the inspection tower that has been erected on the neighbouring edge of the Central Court [I was] tempted in the warm moonlight to look down the staircase-well, [whereupon] the whole place seemed to awake awhile to life and movement. Such was the force of the illusion that the Priest-King with his plumed lily crown, great ladies, tightly girdled, flounced and corseted, long-stoled priests, and, after them, a

When the novelist Henry Miller visited the site in 1939, he declared: "However Knossos may have looked in the past, however it may look in the future, this one which Evans has created is the only one I shall ever know. I am grateful to him for what he did, grateful that he had made it possible for me to descend the grand staircase, to sit on that marvelous throne chair...." Above: The restored throne room.

retinue of elegant but sinewy youths—as if the Cup-
bearer and his fellows had stepped down from the walls
—passed and repassed on the flights below."

This rather poetic dream was a powerful inspiration to
the archaeologist and has left echoes in all his lectures and
newspaper articles. No doubt he hoped through his
restorations to give greater
vividness to ruins that
some have judged as
disappointing. (Here, for
instance, is a remark from
the diary of a well-to-do
Englishwoman who visited
Knossos in 1922, before
the completion of the
restoration in 1930: "There
are many stone staircases
leading into different
chambers, none of which
can really be called palatial;
there is a great number of
terra-cotta vases which
served as temporary storage
for treasures, as well as a
small throne of King Minos:
those are the only items
worth looking at!") As
Charles Picard tellingly
pointed out in an article
defending Evans's work,
"The Knossos that meets
our eye is at once the
Knossos of Minos…and
of Sir Arthur Evans." Conscientiously and scientifically
though Evans worked, the result is, inevitably, a palace
dreamed up by an archaeologist who was very much a man
of his era, influenced by the tastes and methods of his time.

From 1909 on, Evans was showered with honors,
including a knighthood in 1911. Until the last day of his
life, in 1941, he devoted himself to archaeology: Just three
days before his death, when he had long since retired
from Knossos, he discovered a new Roman road on the
outskirts of Oxford.

In this portrait Evans the Edwardian gentleman is surrounded by elements of the Minoan world.

Evans defended his ideas against skeptics with a passion and fury in which we may recognize the ardent liberal and defender of rights who had traveled in Bosnia and Croatia.

The great task

In *The Times* (London) of 31 October 1905 Evans commented on the work upon the grand staircase: "The result achieved by this legitimate process of reconstitution is such that it must appeal to the historic sense of the most unimaginative. To a height of over 25 feet [7½ meters] there rise before us the Grand Staircase and columnar hall of approach practically unchanged since they were traversed 3½ millenniums back by kings and queens of Minos' stock…. We have here all the materials for the reconstruction of a brilliant picture of that remote epoch." The correspondent for the *Journal des Débats* was less enthusiastic: "There are more masons, carpenters, and smiths at work on this task of rebuilding than there are diggers in the excavation field. Everything is being cleaned up, dressed up, completed."

Before and after

The French poet Henri de Régnier visited Knossos in 1904. He produced a lengthy article on the discoveries for the paper *Gaulois du Dimanche*, exclaiming: "A magician has struck the ground with his wand and the ancient residence of the old Cretan king has come back to life." The west wing (in its state in 1900, above) was reconstructed several times, the last in 1930 (below): at right is the throne room, with the staircase placed at left and the floor of an upper story rebuilt in cement. The space above the throne room was used for exhibitions of reproductions of frescoes found on the site. Evans was eager to display objects unearthed during the dig and did so in the queen's apartments and the south propylaeum.

"The royalty of the fleur-de-lys, the virgin mother, Our Lady of the Mountain or of the Waves, the plastic symbols, the number three or the cross, the 'Parisienne' of Knossos, the boxers, and toreadors bring very close to us a life separated from our own by thousands of years."

Henri Berr
preface to Gustave Glotz's
The Aegean Civilisation
1925

CHAPTER V
MINOAN ART NOUVEAU

The modern world was fascinated by the Cretan discoveries, for both their exoticism and their surprising familiarity, which together presented a sort of ideal image of a modern-day antiquity. Knossos as restored by Evans was influenced by Art Nouveau (right: A vase with a marine design; opposite: The north entrance).

In scientific circles Evans's discoveries caused great excitement. In 1907 René Dussaud wrote in the *Gazette des Beaux-Arts*: "It is understandable that, through the revelations they have produced as well as by their methodical, rapid execution, the excavations in Crete have inspired unanimous admiration.... They constitute the foremost archaeological accomplishment of the early twentieth century."

The news spread with remarkable speed, greatly aided by Evans himself. During each year's excavation season, from approximately March through June, he received many visitors, historians and archaeologists, whom he showered with information about the latest discoveries.

In the words of one specialist, Crete has become "a place of pilgrimage for archaeologists." Duncan Mackenzie recorded in his notebook, sometimes in humorous terms, the arrival of one or another specialist to whom Evans was obliged to do the honors of the site. Below: The west court during excavations at Knossos.

Among the dozens of guests, famous or otherwise, were Wilhelm Dörpfeld, Schliemann's associate at Troy, for whom Evans organized a Cretan festival in 1903 in the freshly cleared theater area; Edmond Pottier, associate curator of oriental antiquities at the Louvre, who came to Knossos in January 1901 and published on his return a long, picturesque account along with a historical analysis of Minoan civilization; and Father M.-J. Lagrange of the Catholic order of Preaching Brothers, a correspondent of the French Institute who visited the ruins on behalf of readers of the *Revue Biblique* in October 1906.

On his return to England each year Evans spent the summer writing copious reports that he published in

Visits by Dörpfeld, one of the archaeologists of Troy, inspired special comments in Mackenzie's notebook. Dörpfeld's remarks seem to have played an important part in the other archaeologists' understanding of the Minoan ruins at the beginning of the excavation.

scholarly journals. He gave frequent lectures at the
Society of Anthropology, the Society of Antiquaries,
the Ashmolean Museum, and elsewhere. Throughout
Europe and America specialized periodicals closely
followed the discoveries with well-illustrated
articles. The learned world, very classical in its training
at that period, had begun to consider questions of Greek
prehistory only after the revelations of Schliemann. Now
all the scholarly writings of Evans's contemporaries
expressed the same astonishment at the discovery of
an Aegean civilization forty centuries old.

Crete in the headlines

Evans's discoveries also excited the wider public. He
wrote numerous summaries of his work for the English
press, particularly *The Times* and the *Guardian*, reprinted
in American papers. As a former reporter, he was adept
at presenting the surprises of the dig, highlighting
picturesque details of life on the site, painting the
Cretan landscape, describing the damage caused by an

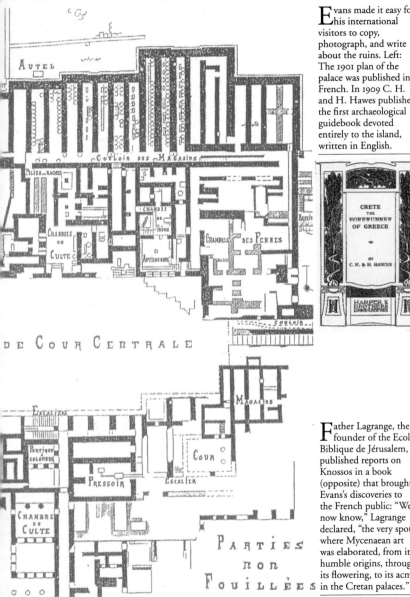

Evans made it easy for his international visitors to copy, photograph, and write about the ruins. Left: The 1901 plan of the palace was published in French. In 1909 C. H. and H. Hawes published the first archaeological guidebook devoted entirely to the island, written in English.

Father Lagrange, the founder of the Ecole Biblique de Jérusalem, published reports on Knossos in a book (opposite) that brought Evans's discoveries to the French public: "We now know," Lagrange declared, "the very spot where Mycenaean art was elaborated, from its humble origins, through its flowering, to its acme in the Cretan palaces."

Jazz, Corsets and Bathtubs in

earthquake. His dramatic flair was also evident in his preference for labeling the various palace rooms with evocative and sometimes inappropriate names, rather than numerals, as was, and is, standard practice: hall of the double axes, corridor of the procession, initiation room, queen's megaron, grand staircase, and, outside the palace, house of the fallen blocks, house of the high priest, house of the chancel screen, or the caravanserai.

All the major popular and prestigious European newspapers sent reporters and devoted many articles to the work in progress.

Curiosity seekers descended on Knossos en masse. Among the first arrivals were the British forces stationed at Heraklion, whom Doll received for tea under the olive trees; later came cruise ships of all nations on their way to Egypt or Lebanon.

Old Knossos 5000 Years Ago

Thus, between 1900 and 1910, not a year passed without a review or a mass-circulation daily paper reporting the news of "revolutionary discoveries in Crete": In quick succession the throne of Minos, the

This was the headline in the *American Weekly* of 13 November 1922, reporting the discoveries at Knossos. "The Fairy Tale of Ancient Crete," "A Vanished Empire," "The Inexhaustible Earth of Crete," "Was Minos Jewish?"—the headlines yelled in the international press from Athens to Melbourne and from Geneva to New York. A photographic atlas of the Cretan antiquities was popular throughout Europe.

Vase Bearer fresco, the sarcophagus of Hagia Triada, the grand staircase of the east wing, the *Serpent Goddess.* In 1909 *The Times* even published an article titled "The Lost Continent," in which the author identified Crete with Atlantis.

As public enthusiasm grew, Cretan archaeology was popularized in myriad ways, for example in photographic postcards of the isle's antiquities. Crete became a stopping place for the major cruises. As Pottier noted in 1902, "Each spring for the past three years has brought its processions of tourists, and soon there will be a little *x* beside the museum of Candia in every good Cook's Guide, and one for the ruins of Knossos in the

The discovery of the *Vase Bearer* fresco (below) inspired numerous commentaries in the press. This was the first appearance of a Minoan face and it led some writers immediately to claim Minoan civilization for the West: "One is struck," Pottier declared, "by the purely European appearance of the face; this long, flowing hair, this wide gaze, this straight-nosed profile with its forthright chin recall the Greek ideal more than anything else; the multicolored rosettes of the clothing add an exotic foreign touch; the posture of the torso lends an element of barbarian pride. This is a work imbued with oriental touches, but translated into a 'new spirit.' This is the entry on the world stage of the European." The sensational discovery of Minoan civilization inspired numerous books, such as that by James Baikie (above), published in 1907.

Baedeker." The Baedeker Guide, which ignored Crete in its 1888 volume, devoted fifteen pages to the island in the 1904 edition.

Hour of glory

Evans and his team received other prominent visitors, such as the dancer Isadora Duncan and the poet Henri de Régnier; eminent personalities took tea in the throne room or the hall of colonnades. A museum was opened in Heraklion, looking rather like a shop, according to one traveler, featuring heaps of "archaeological booty, torn still warm and throbbing from the earth; it was an awakening of corpses buried for centuries, whose eyes opened slowly to the light." It fell to a Frenchman, Gaston Arnaud-Jeanti, to finance the construction of the new museum. Under an agreement with the Cretan government, Evans was allowed to export certain items to England and to make castings of others, to enrich the collections of the Ashmolean Museum at Oxford. The

The archaeological discoveries led to new interest in Crete. The Swiss photographer Frédéric Boissonnas captured scenes of traditional life (above). Below: His book of photos.

museums and universities of Europe, particularly in Germany, were very prompt to acquire molds of the most important objects, such as the Harvesters' vase, discovered at Hagia Triada.

An exhibition of Evans's discoveries was organized in London in 1936 to celebrate the fiftieth anniversary of the British School of Athens. The enduring fascination of Minoan Crete led to the rapid appearance, between 1910 and 1940, of forgeries on the art market, especially of Minoan seals and statuettes.

The familiar minoans

Few events in the history of archaeology have aroused such enthusiasm. The phenomenon of Crete's popularity in the public imagination cannot be explained by mere curiosity or even by the sensational nature of some of the discoveries. Something in Minoan art and culture appealed to the modern world. The specialists themselves, starting with Evans, were immediately struck by the modern and familiar nature of this forgotten art. In 1903 Evans compared a fresco fragment from Knossos to the wallpaper designs of William Morris, one of the

Gilliéron's prints of Minoan antiquities, sold throughout Europe by catalogue, were true works of art. They enabled a wide public to study the Heraklion museum's collection (below).

founders of Art Nouveau in England. Similarly, Father Lagrange saw something contemporary in the fresco of a lady in profile, known as the *Parisienne*, for her particularly elegant and sophisticated beauty: "Beyond classical art, so simple in its forms, one rediscovered the modern world, with an elegance at once more familiar and more affected." Concerning the costumes worn by Minoan women in the frescoes, the ever-serious Reinach wrote in 1904: "The women of Knossos in 1600 BC shared with the Parisiennes of our day the notion that a dress should cling around the hips and widen toward the hem." It was hardly surprising, then, that the scholarly Dussaud, in the same breath, censured both Minoan and modern women for the excessive use of corsets to narrow their waistlines.

A prehistoric hygiene lesson

Evans and his contemporaries particularly felt the modernity of the Minoan world in matters of domestic comfort. In the palaces of Knossos and Phaistos archaeologists found a complete system of light shafts that provided illumination and air circulation in the rooms, a sophisticated system of water conduits arranged like waterfalls, their flow regulated for the drainage of rainwater, and modern conveniences like the latrines in the east wing of the palace of Minos, which left visitors speechless.

The fresco known as the *Parisienne* was an overnight sensation, as Pottier testifies: "Her disheveled hair, the provocative 'kiss curl' on her forehead, her enormous eye and sensual mouth, stained a violent red in the original, her tunic with its blue, red, and black stripes, the mass of ribbons tossed over her shoulder in a 'come-hither' gesture, this mixture of naive archaism and spicy modernism, this quick sketch traced by a paintbrush on a wall at Knossos more than three thousand years ago to give us the impression of a Daumier or a Degas, this Pasiphaë who looks like an habitué of Parisian bars —everything about this work conspires to amaze us; in sum, there is something about the discovery of this unheard-of art that we find stunning, even scandalous."

A bourgeois level of modern comfort, indeed of perfected luxury is found throughout the site, even in the common homes in such towns as Tylissos and Palaikastro. The archaeologists were continually amazed at what they found. Maxime Collignon spoke with astonishment of the pleasant, comfortable quality of the rooms, especially the royal apartments; there were a sitting room with adjustable partitions, bathrooms, "water reservoirs to cool the rooms," a veranda commanding a vast panorama, all of it decorated with care. Adolphe Reinach goes further still: "Above the porticos of his courtyards Minos raised as many as three stories, reached by a tangle of staircases and corridors; beside the great throne rooms and the paved areas surrounded by ramps for bull running or dancing, the baths and even *lavatories* answer our hygienic needs."

This comfort and refinement were particularly surprising because in the early twentieth century the middle classes of Europe had themselves not known such comforts for long. The Minoan world therefore seemed resolutely modern. In this connection, Evans recalled two Cretan legends: It was in this kingdom that aviation was invented by Daedalus and Icarus and that the first robot was designed, in the form of an animated bronze statue!

Art Nouveau on Crete

This sense of familiarity led the specialists to associate Minoan art

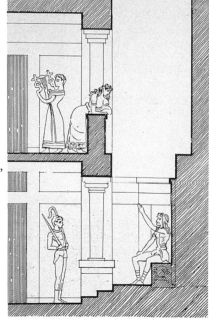

with European Art Nouveau, then a new and exciting art style characterized by rich patterns and colors, sinuous lines, and floral motifs. In 1909 Collignon wrote of a prehistoric mural: "[This frieze] representing lilies painted in white on a red ground would harmonize

This royal gaming table is the best example of Minoan art's mixture of materials: plaster, faience, ivory, crystal, and gold.

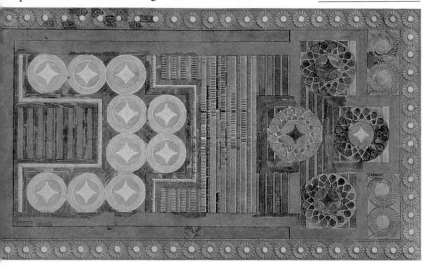

quite well with our [Art Nouveau] wall hangings." In 1932 Picard coined the phrase "pre-modern style for archaeologists" to describe this art risen from oblivion. Like the modern practitioners of Art Nouveau (who were surely influenced by the discoveries on Crete), the Minoans were fond of mixing materials, painting in strong, solid colors, and decorating walls from floor to ceiling. Minoan pottery is richly ornamented with paint or clay paste, often in the curling, intricate designs that so appealed to Art Nouveau artists. The Minoans had a large repertoire of motifs borrowed from nature, especially marine and vegetal themes, flowers and birds.

This predilection for nature, for ornamentation and strong color, seems to stand in opposition to the norms of classical art—or at any rate to the traditional notion of Hellenic art as pure, plain, symmetrical, and unpainted. Pottier wrote: "To make a sky, to make

Minoan architecture provided modern amenities, as illustrated at left by the controlled cascade of water that ran along a stairway in the east wing of the palace, and by the system of light shafts in the royal villa. Such sophisticated engineering offers proof of the civilized nature of the world of Minos. J. C. Stobart notes, in *The Glory that Was Greece*: "The world did not reach the Minoan standard of cleanliness again until the great English sanitary movement of the late nineteenth century."

trees or flowing water—this is something the Greeks
have completely lost in their intransigent love for human
form. Like that of Chaldea and Assyria, the art of Crete
is concerned with nature; Cretan
art loves nature for herself; it
understands her poetry and her
beauty. This too brings it very
close to us." Minoan art
reminded contemporary
artists that the canons
of classicism were
not the only criteria
for artistic creation;
for even in Greece
a civilization before
the classical age had
produced a beauty based
on asymmetry, rich color,
elaborate ornamentation, and
linear decorative motifs. To the
surprise of everyone, the Minoans had already invented
a style that we might comfortably call modern.

An influence in reverse

Thus, Minoan art appeared to have much in common
with modern decorative-art style, and it has been
suggested that the development of Art Nouveau owes
something to the discovery of the Knossos frescoes and
painted ceramics. But the connection between Minoan
art and Art Nouveau is not so simple. Art Nouveau
first appeared in Europe in the mid-nineteenth century,
whereas Minoan art was unknown until 1900. Yet we
may speak of an influence in reverse: The theory of Art
Nouveau, as articulated by John Ruskin or William
Morris, influenced the understanding and interpretation
of Minoan art in somewhat the same way that abstract
art permitted a new, more appreciative view of archaic
Greek or African sculpture.

Berr writes, in his preface to Glotz's *The Aegean
Civilisation* (1925): "The Aegeans, who brought into art
everything, also cultivated the arts properly so called.
They had leisure and they embellished it." Compare

The close affinity between Minoan art and Art Nouveau was widely noticed. Charles Picard wondered, as late as 1932, why more was not made of this aspect of the Knossos frescoes: "Our period might have better recognized, contrary to chronology, as it were, that certain technical tastes were close to our own. [Modern artists] might gladly have co-signed some of these landscapes, with their languid arabesques of twining vegetal decoration." Artists of both periods made frequent use of marine motifs. Opposite: A vase with an octopus design and floral details from Palaikastro; above: A fresco in two horizontal bands from the caravanserai at Knossos; below: Art Nouveau wallpaper by A. H. Mackmurdo, 1884.

this with a comment by William Morris: "Decorative art pursues a dual objective: to make people find pleasure in using the things they must necessarily use, and to make people find as much pleasure in producing the objects they are obliged to produce."

Art Nouveau before 1900 promoted and praised the work of the free artisan over that of the ancient slave or the modern industrial machine. It encouraged artistic virtuosity and individualism in the creation of objects of everyday use; in the eyes of the art historians of the time, the artisans of the Minoan world seemed to have shared this view, and therefore to be kindred spirits.

Knossos, a monument of the twentieth century…. AD

Perhaps this helps us to understand why Evans devoted himself to large-scale restorations. Because Minoan art seemed so modern and familiar, its restoration appeared to pose no particular problems. Evans was encouraged to fill the void left by the absence of trustworthy descriptive textual sources from the Minoan period and to repair the oblivion into which the kingdom of Minos had fallen, relying to a degree on this sense of familiarity to guide him in his choices, rather than on strict scientific method. The result is part reconstruction, part fanciful reinvention.

With its battery of storerooms and its central courtyard, its columns and floors of cement, its too-bright paintings and almost gaudy air, the reconstructed palace of Knossos today testifies to more than the ceremonial architecture of the Minoans in the eighteenth century BC. It speaks as well of the status of archaeological knowledge and taste at the beginning of the twentieth century AD. A

Like their comrades in the twentieth century, Minoan artisans produced objects that were technical marvels, such as this rock-crystal *rhyton* from Zakro.

veritable monument of Art Nouveau, Evans's restoration belongs to the architectural legacy of the turn of the century, with Antoní Gaudí's Park Güell in Barcelona or Josef Hoffmann's Palais Stoclet in Brussels. Its continuing restoration, which has become a necessity in recent years, will have to take this dual artistic heritage into account.

Modern cement, brick, and iron girders, all used by Evans in his restorations, were the preferred materials of Art Nouveau architects. Overleaf: North entrance to the palace of Knossos.

DOCUMENTS

THESEUS AT KNOSSOS

"Picture to yourself all the king's palaces you ever saw, set side by side and piled on one another. That will be a little house, beside the House of the Ax. It was a palace within whose bounds you could have set a town. It crowned the ridge and clung to its downward slopes, terrace after terrace, tier after tier of painted columns, deep glowing red, tapering in towards the base, and ringed at head and foot with that dark brilliant blue the Cretans love. Behind them in the noonday shadow were porticoes and balconies gay with pictured walls, which glowed in the shade like beds of flowers. The tops of tall cypresses hardly showed above the roofs of the courts they grew in. Over the highest roof-edge, sharp-cut against the deep blue Cretan sky, a mighty pair of horns reared towards heaven....

The Palace stood on an easy slope; yet it had no more walls than a common dwelling-house might have, to keep thieves out and slaves in. The roofs were even without battlements, crowned only by their insolent horns, a pair facing each way. Such was the power of Minos. His walls were on the waters, which his ships commanded."

Mary Renault
The King Must Die,
1958

In the Labyrinth

Crete holds a special place in Greek mythology. Its mountains sheltered many gods, goddesses, and monsters. The island is associated with the birth and amorous escapades of Zeus, chief of the Olympian gods, and with the legends of King Minos and the hero Theseus.

The Labyrinth, as imagined in a seventeenth-century print.

The legend of Minos

At his birth the god Zeus was hidden in a cave on Mount Ida or Dikte in the heart of Crete. Indeed, his father, the Titan Kronos, fearful of being supplanted, had the sinister habit of devouring the children borne to him by Rhea, his wife. She managed, however, to conceal the infant Zeus and entrusted him to the Curetes, semidivine sons of the earth and inventors of herding and artisanship. She taught them to dance noisily while striking their shields, to mask the cries of the newborn child from his father's ears. Zeus was nourished by the she-goat Amalthea and as an adult killed his father, as he had feared, and overthrew the Titans. Zeus lived on Olympus but returned to Crete in the form of a bull, with Europa, mortal daughter of the

The Athenians Delivered to the Minotaur, by Gustave Moreau.

king of Phoenicia, whom he had abducted. She bore him three sons, Minos, Rhadamanthys, and Sarpedon.

Minos supplanted his brothers and reigned over Crete with authority, extending his empire far and wide. A scrupulous lawgiver, he also attracted the greatest artists to his court, including Daedalus, the famed architect and engineer. To protect the island's coasts from pirates, Zeus gave the king a great bronze statue capable of movement. Known as Talos, this robot was animated by a divine liquid that circulated through its body in a single artificial vein—an allegory of the invention of bronze casting. Minos, however, committed the error of refusing to sacrifice to the god of the

sea, Poseidon, a bull that he considered too fine to kill.

In punishment the god cast a spell on Pasiphaë, the king's wife, who fell in love with the bull. She had Daedalus construct the hollow statue of a heifer, in which she could conceal herself. In this guise she conceived with the bull the monstrous Minotaur, half human, half animal. In his fury, the king commanded Daedalus to build the Labyrinth as an enclosure to contain the creature. It came to symbolize the tyranny the king exercised over the Aegean peoples; the Athenians, Crete's mainland rivals, were required to surrender seven young men and seven young women as sacrifices to the imprisoned monster every nine years.

Europa abducted by Zeus in the form of a bull. Opposite: Theseus slays the Minotaur.

This terrible tribute was paid regularly until the day when Theseus, son of the king of Athens, volunteered to go to Crete as one of the victims. There he seduced Ariadne, daughter of Minos and Pasiphaë, who gave him a skein of thread to guide him through the corridors of the Labyrinth and a magic sword with which to fight the Minotaur. Theseus killed the monster and freed the young Athenians. He fled with Ariadne, but abandoned her on the way back to Athens on the isle of Naxos. King Minos, angered by this deception and blaming the architect of the Labyrinth, imprisoned Daedalus and his son Icarus in it; they escaped, however, by constructing mechanical wings of wax and feathers. Minos pursued Daedalus to Sicily, only to perish at the hands of King Kokalos, who had him thrust into a bath of

boiling water. The bones of Minos were reportedly found in the fifth century BC by the tyrant Abragas, who returned them to Crete.

Today we can see these myths as an inseparable mixture of fact and fiction, reflecting distant memories of the power and wealth of Crete during the Bronze Age. They were the source material for Homer and writers after him, used to justify or condemn the domination of one city or state over others.

Alexandre Farnoux

The Greek myths have been retold and interpreted by many authors, from Shakespeare to Racine to Freud. Here are two literary accounts of the Cretan story, the first by an Englishman.

The *Blue Bird* fresco, found at Knossos, presents the image of a tranquil world.

When Zeus left Europe, after having fathered Minos, Rhadamanthys, and Sarpedon on her in Crete, she married Asterius, the reigning king, whose father Tectamus son of Dorus had brought a mixed colony of Aeolian and Pelasgian settlers to the island and there married a daughter of Cretheus the Aeolian....

After Asterius's death, Minos claimed the Cretan throne and, in proof of his right to reign, boasted that the gods would answer whatever prayer he offered them. First dedicating an altar to Poseidon, and making all preparations for a sacrifice, he then prayed that a bull might emerge from the sea. At once, a dazzlingly-white bull swam ashore, but Minos was so struck by its beauty that he sent it to join his own herds, and slaughtered another instead. Minos's claim to the throne was accepted by every Cretan, except Sarpedon who, still grieving for Miletus, declared that it had been Asterius's intention to divide the kingdom equally between his three heirs; and, indeed, Minos himself had already divided the island into three parts, and chosen a capital for each....

Meanwhile, Minos had married Pasiphaë, a daughter of Helius and the nymph Crete, otherwise known as Perseis. But Poseidon, to avenge the affront offered him by Minos, made Pasiphaë fall in love with the white bull which had been withheld from sacrifice. She confided her unnatural passion to Daedalus, the famous Athenian crafts-man, who now lived in exile at Cnossus, delighting Minos and his family with the animated wooden dolls he carved for them. Daedalus promised to help her, and built a hollow wooden cow, which he upholstered with a cow's hide, set on wheels concealed in its hooves, and pushed into the meadow near Gortys, where Poseidon's bull was grazing under the oaks among Minos's cows. Then, having shown Pasiphaë how to open the folding doors in the cow's back, and slip inside with her legs thrust down into its hindquarters, he discreetly retired. Soon the white bull ambled up and mounted the cow, so that Pasiphaë had all her desire, and later gave birth to the Minotaur, a monster with a bull's head and a human body.

But some say that Minos, having annually sacrificed to Poseidon the best bull in his possession, withheld his gift one year, and sacrificed merely the next best; hence Poseidon's wrath; others say that it was Zeus whom he offended; others again, that Pasiphaë had failed for several years to propitiate Aphrodite, who now punished her with this monstrous lust. Afterwards, the bull grew savage and devastated the whole of Crete, until Heracles captured and brought it to Greece, where it was eventually killed by Theseus.

Minos consulted an oracle to know how he might best avoid scandal and conceal Pasiphaë's disgrace. The response was: 'Instruct Daedalus to build you a retreat at Cnossus!' This Daedalus did, and Minos spent the remainder of his life in the inextricable maze called the Labyrinth, at the very heart of which he concealed Pasiphaë and the Minotaur....

Rhadamanthys, renowned as a just and upright law-giver, inexorable in his punishment of evildoers, legislated both for the Cretans and for the islanders of Asia Minor, many of whom voluntarily adopted his judicial code. Every ninth year, he would visit Zeus's cave and bring back a new set of laws, a custom afterwards followed by his brother Minos. But some deny that Rhadamanthys was Minos's brother, and call him a son of Hephaestus; as others deny that Minos was Zeus's son, making him the son of Lycastus and the nymph of Ida. He bequeathed land in Crete to his son Gortys, after whom the Cretan city is named....

The triumph of Minos, son of Zeus, over his brothers refers to the Dorians' eventual mastery of Crete, but it was Poseidon to whom Minos sacrificed the bull, which again suggests that the earlier holders of the title "Minos" were Aeolians. Crete had for centuries been a very rich country and, in the late eighth century BC, was shared between the Achaeans, Dorians, Pelasgians, Cydonians (Aeolians), and..."true Cretans."

Minos's palace at Cnossus was a complex of rooms, ante-rooms, halls, and corridors in which a country visitor might easily lose his way. Sir Arthur Evans suggests that this was the Labyrinth, so called from the *labrys*, or double-headed axe; a familiar emblem of Cretan sovereignty—shaped like a waxing and a waning moon joined together back to back, and symbolizing the creative as well as the destructive power of the goddess. But the maze at Cnossus had a separate existence from the palace; it was a true maze...and seems to have been marked out in mosaic on a pavement as a ritual dancing pattern....

Robert Graves
The Greek Myths, vol. 1,
1955

The second account is by an Italian:

In any Cretan story, there's a bull at the beginning and a bull at the end. At the beginning Minos summons Poseidon's white bull up out of the sea. If it appears, he promises, he will sacrifice it to the god. The bull does appear, but Minos doesn't keep his promise. The bull is too beautiful, he doesn't want to kill it, he wants it for his own. It is for that bull that Minos's wife Pasiphaë will develop her fatal passion.

At the end, Theseus captures a bull at Marathon, and once again it's the Cretan bull risen from the sea. After its couplings with Pasiphaë the bull had turned wild, and Minos had called for Heracles to capture it. The hero caught the bull and took it away to the mainland. For a long time the bull wandered about the Peloponnese before turning up in Attica. Where nobody had been able to get the better of it, not even Androgeus, Minos's son, who used to beat all the Athenians in their games. Theseus captured it, at Marathon. He offered it to his father, Aegeus, who sacrificed it to Apollo. Everything between that beginning and that end, which is to say Ariadne's destiny, takes place within the displacement of a sacrifice: from Poseidon to Apollo, from Crete to Athens. That passage is strewn with corpses. The mute, the sacrificial victim is part and parcel of the religious rite. But the myth claims other victims for itself, those who fall around the place of sacrifice, iron filings in the magnetic field. Out of the sacrifice, together with the blood, stream the stories. Thus the characters in the tragedy emerge. In the Cretan stories these characters are Pasiphaë, the Minotaur, Ariadne, Phaedra, Minos, Hippolytus, and Aegeus himself. Returning from Crete, Theseus forgets to lower the black sails, and Aegeus kills himself by leaping from the Acropolis. It's the last footnote to the displacement of the sacrifice....

Mythical figures live many lives, die many deaths, and in this they differ from the characters we find in novels, who can never go beyond the single gesture. But in each of these lives and deaths all the others are present, and we can hear their echo. Only when we become aware of a sudden consistency between incompatibles can we say we have crossed the threshold of myth....

"People say there is a sacred cave in Crete, a cave inhabited by bees, where, as myth would have it, Rhea gave birth to Zeus. There is a sacred law that no one, whether man or god, may set foot there. Every year, at a certain time, a dazzling flame flashes from the cave. The myth says this happens when the blood

Zeus spilled at birth periodically boils. The cave is inhabited by the sacred bees who fed Zeus as a baby. Laius, Celeus, Cerberus, and Egolius took the risk of going into the cave in the hope of stealing a big store of honey; they had protected themselves with bronze armor and began to take the honey; then they saw Zeus's swaddling clothes and their armor began to split across their bodies. Zeus thundered and brandished his lightning bolt, but the Moirai and Themis held him back; the holiness of the place would have suffered had someone died there; so Zeus turned the intruders into birds; and they became the progenitors of those species which bear omens: the solitary sparrow, the green woodpecker, the cerberus, and the barn owl. When any of these birds appear, they offer truer and better omens than other birds, because they have seen the blood of Zeus" [Antoninus Liberalis, *Metamorphoses*, XIX].

Zeus's birthplace, the Cretan cave, was thus out of bounds to both gods and men. And it was the place where one could not die. That cave held a secret beyond any other. When a rite is secret, it is so because in this way it "imitates the nature of the divine, which eludes our perception" [Strabo, *Geography*, X]. But here the divine wished to elude even the perception of the gods. What was it that Zeus had to conceal from the other gods at all costs? The four young Cretans stepped into a dark space

This fresco from the corridor of the procession is almost entirely a reconstruction; it depicts the power of Minos.

dripping with sweetness. The rock was spread thick with honey. The honey stuck to the rock the way their bodies stuck to their bronze armor. In the shadows they noticed some bloody swaddling clothes. When he opened his eyes at birth, these same rocks had been the first thing Zeus saw. He was like any baby then: "stained with blood and with the waters of his mother's womb, more like someone just killed than someone just born" [Plutarch, "On the Love of Offspring," *Moralia*]. The four young Cretans were thinking about this, about those bloodstains in the honey—might there have been a murder?—when they felt their bronze armor splitting apart. Zeus thundered. There was a great light.

In Crete the secret had always been there for everybody to see. Up on a mountain they would show people Zeus's tomb. They told the truth one must not tell. No one believed them. Ever after, people would say: Cretans, liars all....

> Roberto Calasso
> *The Marriage of*
> *Cadmus and Harmony,*
> 1993

Daedalus: the first artist

The mythical Daedalus is credited with designing the Labyrinth and may therefore be said to be the legendary architect of Knossos. In addition he is said to have invented a set of mechanical wings, the steam bath, the folding chair, marvelous children's toys, and some of the tools of carpentry and architecture: the plumb line, the compass, the toothed saw, the auger, the axe, and glue. His sculptures were renowned for their ingenious mechanics and lifelike quality (for example, the mechanical bull in which Pasiphaë hid); Talos, the walking statue that guarded

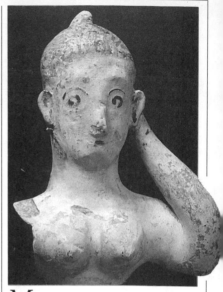

Minoan statuette, fourteenth century BC.

Crete, is sometimes said to have been made by him and sometimes by the smith-god Hephaestus. The connection between artistic genius and godlike powers is thus one of the most ancient ideas of the west.

Talos was also the name of Minos's bull-headed bronze servant, given him by Zeus to guard Crete. Some say that he was a survivor of the brazen race who sprang from the ash-trees; others, that he was forged by Hephaestus in Sardinia, and that he had a single vein which ran from his neck down to his ankles, where it was stoppered by a bronze pin. It was his task to run thrice daily around the island of Crete and throw rocks at any foreign ship; and also to go thrice yearly, at a more leisurely pace, through the villages of Crete, displaying Minos's laws inscribed on brazen tablets. When the

Sardinians tried to invade the island, Talos made himself red-hot in a fire and destroyed them all with his burning embrace, grinning fiercely....

Hephaestus is sometimes described as Hera's son by Talos, and Talos as Daedalus's young nephew;...such chronological discrepancies are the rule in mythology. Daedalus ("bright" or "cunningly wrought"), Talos ("sufferer"), and Hephaestus ("he who shines by day"), are shown by the similarity of their attributes to be merely different titles of the same mythical character....

In one sense the labyrinth from which Daedalus and Icarus escaped was the mosaic floor with the maze pattern, which they had to follow in the ritual partridge dance; but Daedalus's escape to Sicily, Cumae, and Sardinia refers perhaps to the flight of the native bronze-workers from Crete as the result of successive Hellenic invasions....

Talos is said by Hesychius to be a name for the Sun; originally, therefore, Talos will have coursed only once a day around Crete. Perhaps, however, the harbours of Crete were guarded against pirates by three watches which sent out patrols. And since Talos the Sun was also called Taurus...his thrice-yearly visit to the villages was probably a royal progress of the Sun-king, wearing his ritual bull-mask—the Cretan year being divided into three seasons. Talos's red-hot embrace may record the human burnt sacrifices offered to Moloch, *alias* Melkarth, who was worshipped at Corinth as Melicertes, and probably also known in Crete. Since this Talos came from Sardinia, where Daedalus was said to have fled when pursued by Minos, and was at the same time Zeus's present to Minos, the mythographers have simplified the story by giving

Hephaestus, rather than Daedalus, credit for its construction; Hephaestus and Daedalus being the same character....

Talos's single vein belongs to the mystery of early bronze casting by the *cire-perdue* method. First, the smith made a beeswax image which he coated with a layer of clay, and laid in an oven. As soon as the clay had been well baked he pierced the spot between heel and ankle, so that the hot wax ran out and left a mould, into which molten bronze could be poured. When he had filled this, and the metal inside had cooled, he broke the clay, leaving a bronze image of the same shape as the original wax one. The Cretans brought the *cire-perdue* method to Sardinia, together with the Daedalus cult. Since Daedalus learned his craft from Athene, who was known as Medea at Corinth, the story of Talos's death may have been a misreading of an icon which showed Athene demonstrating the *cire-perdue* method. The tradition that melted wax caused Icarus's death seems to belong, rather, to the myth of his cousin Talos; because Talos the bronze man is closely connected with his namesake, the worker in bronze and the reputed inventor of compasses.

Compasses are part of the bronze-worker's mystery, essential for the accurate drawing of concentric circles when bowls, helmets, or masks have to be beaten out. Hence Talos was known as Circinus, "the circular," a title which referred both to the course of the sun and to the use of the compass. His invention of the saw has been rightly emphasized: the Cretans had minute double-toothed turning-saws for fine work, which they used with marvellous dexterity.

Robert Graves
The Greek Myths, vol. I,
1955

The return of the Minotaur

Even more than Heinrich Schliemann's discoveries on the Greek and Turkish mainland, the excavation of Knossos stirred great public interest. Echoes of Cretan art influence reverberated through the first half of the twentieth century, inspired directly by the Minoan finds and arising from a renewed fascination with the legends of the Cretan cycle.

The *Enigma of Atlantis,* by Edgar P. Jacobs.

The Labyrinth rediscovered

After Evans's discovery of Knossos, numerous literary works mentioned the resurrected kingdom of Minos. In Marcel Proust's novel *Within a Budding Grove* (1918), for instance, we read: "Geographers or archaeologists may conduct us over Calypso's island, and may excavate the Palace of Minos. Only, Calypso becomes then a mere woman, Minos a mere king with no semblance of divinity." In *The Guermantes Way* (1920), Proust refers more specifically to the palace of Knossos: "Laid out in quincunxes, these [orchards]...formed great quadrilaterals—separated by low walls —of white blossom, on each side of which the light fell differently, so that all these airy roofless chambers seemed to belong to a Palace of the Sun, such as one might find in Crete...." His information seems to have come from an article by Maxime Collignon, published in 1909 in the *Gazette des Beaux-Arts.*

Along with these explicit references, we also find Minoan civilization and its discovery associated with the submerged cities and forgotten worlds that haunt explorers' reports and tales of adventure, such as those of H. Rider Haggard and H. P. Lovecraft. Passages in *Atlantis* by Paul Benoît (1919) seem inspired, for instance, by the latest Minoan discoveries, as reported in London by *The Times.* Benoît's ancient palace of Antinéa, last queen of Atlantis, is remarkable for its labyrinthine architecture and presents all the comforts of a Minoan dwelling: light shafts, baths, tiled floors, armchairs, and so on; the queen's apartment seems a deliberate echo of the queen's

Hercules conquers Atlantis in an Italian film.

animated statue Talos, featured in *Jason and the Argonauts* (1963).

The second life of the Minotaur

The Minotaur in particular assumed new importance in the imaginative life of the twentieth century. Evans's discoveries added new luster to his legend; in 1933 the Surrealists adopted the monster as their symbol in a new review of art, archaeology, and ethnology titled *Minotaure*. The monster was an inexhaustible source of inspiration, the incarnation of the "convulsive beauty" of the modern world, and appeared in artworks from Pablo Picasso to André Masson. The Cretan myths also furnished fertile themes in modern literature, influenced, perhaps, by Freud's use of them as paradigms: The Labyrinth and its monstrous tenant symbolized a consciousness in crisis from Laurence Durrell to Jorge Luís Borges, Albert Camus, and Michel Butor. Theseus and Daedalus incarnated heroes, men of action, and creators in the books of Angelos Sikelianos, André Gide, and James Joyce. When the French journal *Les Cahiers du Sud* devoted a special issue to the Greek myths in 1939, more than half the text dealt with the Cretan cycle, with contributions by such authors as Marguerite Yourcenar, who also wrote a play on the theme of the Minotaur. More recently, Carol Christ published *Odyssey with the Goddess: A Spiritual Quest in Crete* (1995). Thus have the Minoans contributed—involuntarily and with many misconstructions—to the history of European consciousness in the twentieth century.

megaron as restored by Evans; while Antinéa herself could be one of the women depicted in the Knossos frescoes: "A type of slender young woman, with wide green eyes, an aquiline profile.... An under-aged Queen of Sheba with a look, a smile never found in the tales of the Orient. A miracle of irony and nonchalance.... She wears a garment that reveals her fine breast." A similar note sounds in more recent historical novels that portray the Minoans, such as *The Egyptian* (1945) by Mika Waltari, *The King Must Die* (1958) and *The Bull from the Sea* (1962) by Mary Renault, and *At the Palaces of Knossos* by the Cretan author Nikos Kazantzakis. E. P. Jacobs used Minoans in comic strips in 1957. And finally, they received rather rough cinematic treatment in such "historical" movies as *Hercules and the Captive Women* (1963) and *The Maze Maker* (1968), directed by M. Ayrton. Filmmakers sometimes turned to Crete for photogenic monsters like the

Alexandre Farnoux

The past informs the present

"Little by little, through continual discoveries, archaeology has succeeded in filling the great gap that still separates the origins of history from the end of the geological periods by working back through the centuries."

Salomon Reinach
La Gazette des Beaux-Arts, 1904

Crete in ancient literature

In addition to influencing art and literature, Cretan history has given the world at least one word: *syncretism,* meaning the reconciliation of conflicting beliefs, or the historical process by which a belief system develops by merging or adapting previous, and sometimes conflicting, practices. The word comes from the Greek word *synkrētizein* (from *syn*=together; *krēte*=Crete), meaning "to unite against a common enemy." It refers to an event, possibly apocryphal, in Cretan history: the formation of a federation of Cretan cities, which had been famous for their hostility to one another. The Greco-Roman writer Plutarch, writing in the first or second century AD, refers to this event as having occurred in earlier antiquity: "The Cretans,…though they often quarrelled with and warred against each other, made up their differences and united when outside enemies attacked; and this it was which they called 'syncretism'" (Plutarch, "On Brotherly Love," *Moralia*).

Elsewhere Plutarch comments that Crete has not been well treated by earlier writers, many of whom came from Athens, Knossos's rival: "Verily, it seems to be a grievous thing for a man to be at enmity with a city which has a language and a literature. For Minos was always abused and reviled in the [Athenian] theatres, and it did not avail him that Hesiod called him 'most royal,' or that Homer styled him 'a confidant of Zeus,' but the…poets prevailed, and from platform and stage showered obloquy down upon him, as a man of cruelty and violence. And yet they say that Minos was a king and lawgiver.…" (Plutarch, "Theseus," *Parallel Lives*).

Above: The Mu district of the dig at Mallia. Below: Vases *in situ* in the Nu area.

Archaeology and imagination

A great deal of work has been done since Evans's time on the Minoan frescoes, which are the oldest examples of Greek painting. The discovery of more new images, fresco fragments, seal stones, and decorated vases has further enriched our knowledge of Minoan iconography and has led to new interpretations. Two archaeologists examine some of this new research.

It is high time…to remind ourselves that imagination can be dangerous, leading us into errors that can be difficult to rectify. Minoan archaeology has known its share of famous examples.

Let's begin with one of the simplest. It serves to illustrate the basic ambiguity inherent in reading any document. A Minoan seal stone, known from imprints discovered in a treasury of the palace of Knossos, bore an unusual image. Evans, and later the Reverend Victor Kenna, a contemporary expert on Minoan and Mycenaean glyptics, saw it as depicting three trees, three poplars blowing in the wind, an image that showed once again the delicate feeling for nature one associates with the Minoans. A less romantic connoisseur, John Betts, pointed out that, if one rotated the figure by 90 degrees, the supposed poplars could simply become three ships' hulls with raised prow, like those seen on other reproductions of ships. But were the Minoans actually using this type of ship during the period to which the imprints are attributed? The decision may not be so simple after all.

It is sometimes possible to remove any uncertainty through careful observation. This was the case with a fresco Evans presented as depicting a

An imprint from a Minoan seal found at Knossos, viewed in two ways: as three trees or three ships' prows.

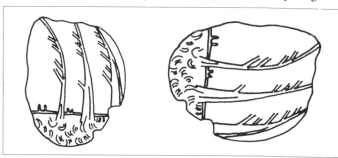

young boy, a prince no doubt, plucking crocuses while walking in the flowering garden of the palace [see page 77]. The painting had been restored by one of the two Gilliérons, father and son, the Swiss artists who collaborated so effectively with Evans. Too effectively, perhaps: They had so fully assimilated Minoan art that they had no hesitation in reconstructing it, reshaping it to their ideas. In any event, much later, while examining the *Saffron Gatherer* in the museum of which he was director, N. Platon noticed that one flower stem was in fact the tail of a blue monkey, and that a ring of crocuses actually belonged to the snout of one of these exotic animals, gamboling among the royal gardens of Knossos. Once the experts had verified and approved Platon's view—and all this occurred after Evans's death, of course, and after the second of the Gilliérons had retired —there was no choice but to have the fresco restored in a form closer to the archaeological truth. The young prince had to make way for a blue monkey.

Continuing in the same vein, Platon decided to reexamine the most famous of the Knossos frescoes, the one that Evans and subsequently the whole world knew and loved as the *Parisienne*. This is the lovely Minoan lady with dark curls fetchingly arranged on her forehead and neck, a pale complexion, a fine profile, and red-painted lips, whom we have already encountered. The painting, a little larger than a miniature fresco, seemed to lie in size between the miniatures and the painting known as *Ladies in Blue,* which had been restored using the miniatures as a model. Only her bust had been preserved, in its tight-fitting, almost transparent garment with delicate embroidery. As

The *Parisienne.*

her title suggests, the elegant lady of Knossos had been completed, somewhat imaginatively, to resemble an urban coquette of the Belle Epoque. But Platon, after studying painted fragments collected at the same time as the *Parisienne,* produced a reconstruction in a much more serious vein. The young woman was seated, just as Evans had assumed, but she was neither a lady of rank nor an elegant commoner. She was a goddess who, along with others, received the homage and offerings of a series of young men and women. Whereas her portrait was supplemented by a few small fragments that had escaped the first reconstruction, the scene as a whole, laid out on two separate levels like certain Egyptian or Mesopotamian paintings, assumed a staid, hieratic air, in which the [repainted] face of our poor Parisienne, with her sparkling eye, seemed almost out of place.

Wisely, the curator [Platon] did not touch this image, which had become so popular since Evans's time. He decided only to place beside her a small graphic reconstruction of the work as it must have looked to Minoans viewing it on the wall.

For false images have sometimes won the lasting affection of the public—acts of imagination that border on fraud, which popular opinion agrees should be condemned—but not removed! Another example is the famous *Prince with Lilies*. At the south entry to the palace of Knossos this imposing figure reportedly led a parade, on two levels, of bearers of offerings in what Evans dubbed the corridor of the procession. Who has not seen this noble silhouette [see page 60], dressed in a simple loincloth, wearing a garland of lilies and a heavy plumed crown, holding on a leash some favored animal—possibly a griffin—as he walks among the flowers? Discovered in fragments in 1901 and reconstructed by the elder Gilliéron, the figure holds a place of honor in the Heraklion Museum, and the tourist is greeted at the palace of Knossos by a reproduction, which Evans placed under the portico of the south entrance, restored by his efforts.

Doubts had been expressed concerning this image for some time, and the younger Gilliéron removed it from the field of lilies imagined by his father, on the model of the great Palace-style storage jars. Evans himself had thought the fragments unconnected. He had attributed the diadem to a king, the torso to a boxer, and the rest of the body to a third male figure. But he had yielded to the temptation to bring them together in one figure, which his two

Above and opposite: the *Prince with Lilies* fresco from Knossos, showing two proposed reconstructions.

artful restorers were happy to display in a triumphant pose at the head of a long procession. Several versions of the scene were proposed, but always with the same prince crowned with lilies, and Evans kept up a stream of detailed descriptions, minutiae, and analyses to justify the reconstruction. Critics questioned the authenticity of the theatrical gesture, the sort and symbolism of the animal held on a leash, and the appropriateness of the headdress to the character, not to mention many other details. In fact, Gilliéron had inpainted flat tones of his own invention to link the ancient fragments he assembled. And the contrast he maintained between the plainness of his additions (the face, tresses, belt, and

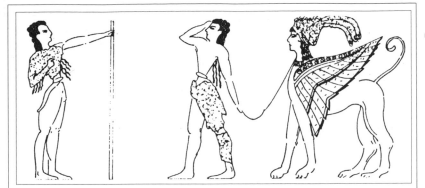

right leg) and the cracked, chipped appearance of the original parts seemed a sign of honesty. But was it?

In 1960 a French archaeologist of our acquaintance, André Dessenne, who was studying Mycenaean ivories in the National Museum at Athens, happened to consult an old catalogue of objects discovered at Mycenae that were not on exhibit. He was surprised by a simple reference to a fragment of *pyxis,* or small round box, decorated with a relief that reminded him of the *Prince with Lilies.* But there the animal on the leash was a sphinx, not a griffin, and this creature, not the man, was wearing the fine crown!

Further progress was made when a physician from Marseilles, an amateur archaeologist named Jean Coulomb, analyzed the treatment of musculature in the Knossos fresco and noticed errors in the famous reconstruction. He pointed out how awkwardly the neck was joined to the torso and how anatomically impossible the pose was....

The latest of these scholars—for the time being—is the German archaeologist Wolf Dietrich Niemeier, an unflappable specialist on Knossos, who follows Platon's example with the *Parisienne.* He interprets the *Prince with Lilies* as the god of eternal youth, ruler of the palace, toward whom the double procession marches along the Knossos corridor. Does it matter that he is flanked by two sphinxes crowned with lilies and plumes, or that this hairstyle belongs, as in other Cretan paintings, to a priestess, here the leader of the parade? Is this an eternally young Zeus or his son Minos? Does it matter? What's represented here is the divine sovereign of Crete.

Why not? Imagination lives.

We should not blame archaeologists [for these flaws], nor Minoan archaeology in general. It is a difficult, painstaking science, hindered by its very wealth of material and by the absence of deciphered texts. It can only progress from one hypothesis to the next—just as do the so-called exact sciences.

All we can demand of the archaeologist is to be reasonable. Not to impose his own hypotheses arbitrarily, especially if there is a risk that they may become too firmly fixed.

M. Van Effenterre
and M. Mastorakis
Les Minoens, 1991

The Minoan world today

Since the death of Arthur Evans, excavations in Crete have continued steadily, and our knowledge of Minoan civilization has been greatly enriched. Research is carried out by an international team: Greeks, British, Americans, Canadians, Swedes, Italians, Frenchmen, Belgians, Spaniards, and Germans all work on the island every year.

Hagia Triada.

Today archaeological work is not restricted to excavating land sites; it includes surface surveying and underwater excavations. Jacques Cousteau, for instance, made dives with his team along the coastlines of the island, searching for sunken sites, while teams of archaeologists have now roamed the unfamiliar regions of

eastern and western Crete. This intense activity has led to the uncovering of hundreds of new structures: a fourth palace was found at Zakro in 1961; the ancient cities of Mallia and Palaikastro are much better understood today, thanks to their systematic exploration; in the 1970s necropolises were excavated at Arkhanes, revealing tombs of royal splendor, and at Armeni, where more than one hundred tombs were explored; Minoan arsenals have been found at Kommos, the port of the palace of Phaistos; and, since 1986, studies have been conducted on the ancient road infrastructure throughout the kingdom of Minos. This wealth of new documentation, however, has not substantially altered the main outlines of Minoan history as they were established by Sir Arthur Evans.

Rural communities

It is generally accepted today that at

Gold jewelry from Mochlos.

the start of the third millennium BC
Crete attracted settlers from the
northeastern coasts of the Aegean.
During the period known as the
Early Minoan (3200–2200 BC) a large
settlement emerged at Knossos,
made up of gradually accruing rooms
devoted to crafts (pottery, weaving)
and to housing for members of the
community. The adjoining terrain was
farmed. The prosperity of eastern Crete
at this early period is indicated by the
wealth of certain tombs, such as one at
Mochlos, where a remarkable set of
gold jewelry was found.

The Minoan palaces

We do not know exactly why the
Minoans built great palaces in Crete.
Whether a local architectural idea or
the result of an external influence,
palaces appeared at several locations on
the island at approximately the same
time, at the beginning of the Middle
Minoan period (2100–1800 BC). Cities
began to appear at the same time, at
Mallia and elsewhere. The palaces
developed in two distinct periods, the
First Palace period (Middle Minoan II,
1800–1700 BC), and the Second Palace
period (Late Minoan I, 1650–1450 BC).
Both periods ended with the wholesale
destruction of the buildings, from
natural causes in the first instance—
probably an earthquake—and through
human agency in the second: Some
believe that the Mycenaeans invaded
Crete and conquered the rich plains
and valleys of the island.

The First and Second Palace
periods saw the flowering of Minoan
civilization around regional centers,
the palaces of Knossos, Phaistos,
Mallia, and Zakro. These palaces were
the sites of administrative authority—
witness the presence of archival
documents—in the service of a power
that was both royal and religious.
Ceremonial rooms, sanctuaries, rich
furnishings, and luxury objects are all
indications that the palaces were the
residences of kings. If Crete was
carved up into independent kingdoms
during the first phase, it is now widely
believed that in the Late Minoan
period the island was consolidated
under one rule, whose capital was the
palace of Knossos.

Crete continued to trade with
the rest of the ancient world,
particularly Egypt and the Near East.
Today specialists emphasize ties with
the Near East, modifying Evans's
thesis, which regarded Egypt as the
great model for Minoan civilization.
The recent discovery of Minoan-style
frescoes on an Egyptian site on the
Nile River delta has reopened the
debate, however.

Religious practices

Minoan religion remains a hotly
contested subject. It inspired—and

Bull's-head *rhyton* from Knossos.

still inspires today—numerous interpretations linked to the study of images and the identification of sanctuaries. Caves, grottoes, and mountains were cult sites, where numerous offerings related to Minoan worship have been found: bronze and terra-cotta figurines, vases, double-headed axes, pairs of horns. Some rooms in palaces and houses were apparently used as cult areas, and were found to contain incense burners, *rhytons,* benches, and small domed altars. One particular type of room, a sort of semibasement surrounded by a balustrade and reached by a staircase, is considered by many to have been a lustral or ceremonial bath, in which the faithful performed a preparatory rite.

It is believed that the Minoan pantheon was composed of the remnants of a former aniconic cult (the cult of the pillar) together with a central female divinity (the mother goddess), whose attributes were snakes or beasts. The Minoan king may have been the presiding priest of the cult. The Minoans seem to have practiced blood sacrifice, as is depicted in a fresco on the sarcophagus found at Hagia Triada. The bull seems to have been the favored victim, and its horns were a common religious symbol. Bull leaping, possibly as part of a religious rite or festival, consisted of acrobatic exercises with the animal (somewhat comparable to an American rodeo or to Spanish bull running) and ended, no doubt, in his sacrifice. Boxing, portrayed in numerous Minoan images, must also have taken place in the context of public feasts. The dove and a lion-headed spirit were also featured in Minoan religious symbolism.

Everyday life and work

Increased research and documentation since 1900 have enabled archaeologists to draw a fairly precise picture of daily life in the Minoan era, particularly in the Middle Minoan period. The walls of houses usually had a stone foundation and a superstructure of brick or earth mixed with rubble, reinforced with beams to resist the island's frequent earthquakes. Floors were of beaten earth, cement, or paving stones. Houses rarely rose to more than two stories, including a terrace. Illumination was provided by light shafts consisting of small colonnaded courtyards open to the sky. Some

Palace-style *pithos,* with a motif of a two-headed axe.

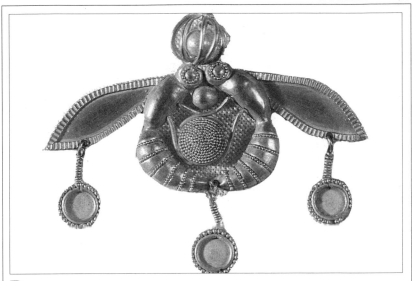

Bee pendant from Mallia.

walls had several doors, forming a kind of movable screen that could be opened or closed at will to regulate temperature and light. In the Late Minoan period, some houses were true villas, luxuriously built of cut stone and decorated with frescoes. On the floors of houses, or fallen from the upper stories, archaeologists often found objects that indicated the function of a room: a metal caster's crucible and mold, a potter's wheel, stone chips left from the carving of seals or stone vases, balances from a weaver's loom, the clay tablets of an archivist, the *pithoi* of a grain storeroom, a carpenter's saw and axe, a wine or oil press, obsidian blades, terra-cotta beehives, a mill for food preparation. Such finds are very useful in establishing the degree of technical development at different periods of Minoan culture. Some products testify to great skill and artisanship: fine stone and crystal vases, ivories composed of separate sections assembled with pegs and animal glue, and granulated goldwork, such as the bee pendant from Mallia. Potters using the quick wheel made cups and vases only a few millimeters thick, while with molds and tinted paste they made composite and polychrome pieces.

The end of a world

Determining the date at which Minoan civilization disappeared is the point where current archaeological research most definitely parts company with Arthur Evans. Evans believed that Minoan civilization had lasted until the Late Minoan I period (1450 BC). In the ruins of the palace of Knossos, he had found hundreds of fragments of tablets inscribed in Linear B, which he believed

Ceremonial axe in the form of a panther, from the palace at Mallia.

belonged to the chancellery of King Minos, as did the older documents written in hieroglyphics and in Linear A. The deciphering of these texts by Michael Ventris and John Chadwick in 1952 proved, however, that this script had been used to write Greek, and was thus the later language of the Mycenaean invaders and of the administration they put in place at Knossos. It was these invaders who had caused the destruction of Minoan civilization in the Late Minoan IB period and who then exploited the island for their own gain. The duration of the Mycenaean kingdom in Crete varies according to the different specialists, and continuing excavations provide fresh information each year. Though they did not attain the prosperity of the kingdom of Minos, it is probable that the Mycenaeans were more than the mere "squatters"

Evans thought them, reoccupying the ruins of cities they had destroyed on their arrival.

Now that the archives of Mycenaean administrators, written in Linear B, have been deciphered, specialists have been able to supplement the archaeological documentation. The tablets record manufacturing activities that have otherwise disappeared, such as animal husbandry and weaving, of which Crete appears to have been a major center. At Se-to-i-ja, a settlement that archaeologists place to the east of Knossos, flocks of sheep were bred for wool and as replacements for animals that were scarce in other villages in the kingdom. We also know that there were workshops for the production of chariots, intended, according to some scholars, to equip the Mycenaean garrison on the island.

Alexandre Farnoux

This finely carved footed stone vessel, found at Hagia Triada, is called the Chieftain Cup. It was at one time thought to represent a prince, and the figure at left is probably aristocratic. The scene is one of a young man's initiation rite; he wears his hair loose and holds out a baton or scepter in a ceremonial pose similar to that seen in the *Vase Bearer* fresco. He faces a helmeted soldier with a sword on his shoulder, behind whom stand ranks of soldiers with huge shields.

The Minoans in the headlines

Minoan archaeology continues to enjoy much press coverage. It still stimulates our imagination, thanks to sensational new discoveries that often remain true to Arthur Evans's extraordinary sense of theater.

The sanctuary of Arkhanes consisted of a storeroom; the cult room, with a statue of the god; and the sacrificial room, where human bones were found. Below: A reconstruction of a sanctuary at Anemosphilia.

Cannibalism in the Minoan paradise?

Recent discoveries in Crete have destroyed the myth of a peaceable, idyllic civilization. In 1979 at Arkhanes, in central Crete, J. and E. Sakellarakis unearthed the remains of a human sacrifice in a Minoan sanctuary. Even more macabre was the discovery by Peter Warren at Knossos one year later: He dug up the bones of two children, aged about eight and eleven, who had been sacrificed and then apparently cut up to be eaten. Press reaction was strong in both cases, as the following 1980 report indicates.

Evans, equipped with his maps, had unearthed the palace of Knossos one step at a time. One of his compatriots, Professor Peter Warren, excavating the basement of a Minoan house [in 1980], made discoveries that will without

doubt revolutionize our knowledge of the Greek world. Although it is still too soon to draw conclusions, we now have evidence that our ancestors tasted human flesh. Professor Warren...is worried not only by his discoveries and what they suggest, but also by the reactions they have elicited. An egotistical chauvinism seems to make many people respond: "Cannibals? Our ancestors? Impossible...."

[Warren's discovery of] human bones has led archaeologists for the first time to consider the possibility of cannibalism in the Minoan era. "They were discovered," Professor Warren stated, "quite by chance in the two cellars of a large, well-built house of dressed stone. In the eastern cellar we found thirty-seven ritual vases decorated with plant motifs, shields, and other Minoan objects.... In the second cellar were many other vases and a fine piece of decorated alabaster.

But that was not all we unearthed.

"We also found bones in the second cellar. Two skulls and 273 bones, belonging to children aged between eight and approximately eleven years. Twenty-five to thirty of these bones bore marks made with a knife.

"What do these knife cuts mean?... Archaeologists have sketched out various hypotheses, none of which has so far been confirmed with any certainty. The scars might have been traces of combat, inflicted by weapons of war. Autopsies showed, however, that the marks were very light, made with caution, one might say. These knife wounds look nothing like those made in the heat of combat.... Moreover, the bones were not connected together, but dispersed and broken. Why?

"It appears," Professor Warren continued, "that the flesh had been removed from the bones like meat when one prepares to cook it, but apparently the operation was not performed by a specialist, such as a butcher or chef of the Minoan era. The most likely hypothesis is that the two children were first sacrificed to the gods and then their flesh was consumed, as was commonly done with sacrificial animals throughout antiquity.

"Professor Binford, an anthropologist, on viewing the photographs of the bones found at the site, agreed with this hypothesis. It is further reinforced by the concurrent discovery of the bones of a sheep that had had its throat cut; the incision at the neck is characteristic of a sacrificial slaughter.

"Thus the hypothesis of cannibalism cannot be ruled out. We refer, of course, to ritual cannibalism. There is no evidence to suggest the existence on Crete of a customary practice of cannibalism, or of the 'forced' cannibalism that may occur out of necessity, when food becomes scarce as a result of a siege or epidemic."

Rena Theoloyidou
Tachydromos, 1980

A god of youth at Palaikastro?

In 1987, excavations at Palaikastro, at the far eastern end of Crete, led the archaeologists Hugh Sackett and Sandy MacGillivray to an extraordinary discovery: a gold and ivory statuette about sixteen inches tall (40.5 cm), dating to the beginning of the Late Minoan period.

Our work at Palaikastro, a site in eastern Crete, has brought us face to face with discoveries that are both fascinating and controversial. Raising "great controversy," however, was not our intention when we began work at Palaikastro in 1986. Nonetheless, when we reflect on the remarkable objects found at the site, our imaginations are irresistibly drawn to the possibility that this late Minoan site was the earliest "home" of the Greek god Zeus.…

Since the turn of the century, when Sir Arthur Evans first discovered the palatial ruins at Knossos, international archaeological efforts at more than 100 sites have helped to reconstruct the Cretan past. Through the study of architecture, artifacts, and burials we have made much progress in piecing together a picture of daily life in Bronze Age Crete. Minoan religion, however, remains one of the most puzzling and difficult aspects of Cretan archaeology.…

Our excavations at Palaikastro have produced unexpected evidence that

suggests that Minoans…worshiped a youthful male divinity whose cult could be the basis for the later Greek cult of the Zeus Kouros, or Zeus as a youth. We have found the largest and finest Minoan ivory sculpture to date; it is of a youthful male, rendered in gold and ivory, the most precious materials available to Minoans.…

The sculpture was unearthed on the very last day of our 1987 season. It was early May, normally a time of sunshine in Crete, but the sky god had devised terrifying thunderstorms the night before, filling the trenches with water and mud. We pumped out the water and dug farther beneath a deep collapse of stone masonry in the plateia. Upon lifting one of the large and well-cut blocks, our foreman, Nikos Dhaskalakis, froze and called for help. He had spotted the ivory torso and one arm of a statuette and small pieces of gold foil.

In 1988 we cleared the rest of the plateia. A few feet from where we had found the ivory torso, we uncovered the top of a stone head rendered in blue-gray serpentine. It was carefully sculptured with a topknot of hair, the sides etched to indicate they had been shaved. We initially wondered if the head might belong to a different statuette, but when the ivory neck was found and attached to the torso, we realized that the several parts were all from the same work. The head was broken into three pieces, perhaps because of a fall during the final conflagration of the buildings. The ivory face most likely splintered into small fragments, most of which have not been recovered. Nonetheless, the remains do show hollow eye sockets. The water-sieving team that processed

The dig at Palaikastro.

all six tons of soil from the area later found two tiny rock-crystal eyes that fit perfectly into the sockets. The sievers also retrieved two exquisitely carved ivory feet....

The exceptional anatomical accuracy and detail of the statuette are astonishing—veins, tendons, and even fingernails are carefully carved as though from life. Such naturalistic treatment is not found again in Greek art until the high Classical period, more than a thousand years later....

The pose, with both fists clenched in front of the chest, is well-known to Minoan iconographers from earlier clay figurines found at the nearby peak sanctuary of Petsophas. These are thought to be votaries, figures assuming a stance of worship, but this pose is also that of a "Youthful God" known from rare representations on Minoan seals....

If the young Minoan initiates worshiped a god in their image—and at their own stage of maturity—as did the later Cretans on the same site, they may have stood before our statuette and chanted a hymn similar to the later "Hymn of the Kouros." The statuette, then, would be the earliest known cult statue of Zeus Kouros.

Hugh Sackett and
Sandy MacGillivray
Archaeology,
September–October 1989

A stone table for sacrificial offerings, from the palace at Mallia.

Forgers in the realm of Minos

Production of Minoan forgeries testifies to the popularity of Cretan archaeology. Evans himself was deceived more than once, notably by the famous forged "treasure of Thisbe." This anecdote by Sir Leonard Woolley, a British archaeologist who visited Evans at Knossos, is one of the rare testimonies available on this important subject.

In Crete in the early years of this century I was stopping with Arthur Evans when he was excavating at Knossos, and one day he got a message from the police at Candia asking him to come to the police station, so we went together—he, Duncan Mackenzie who was his assistant, and myself. And the most surprising thing had happened.

Evans for years had employed two Greeks to restore the antiquities which he had found. They were extraordinarily clever men—an old man and a young one—and he had trained them, and they had worked under the artist whom he employed there, and they had done wonderful restorations for him. Then the old man got ill and at last the doctor told him he was going to die.

He said, "Are you sure?" The doctor said, "Yes, I'm afraid there's no hope for you at all."

"Right," he said. "Send for the police." The doctor said, "You mean the priest?" "No I don't," he said. "I mean the police." He insisted, and they sent for the police, and the police came and asked him, "What on earth do you want?"

"Now I can tell you," said the sick man. "I'm going to die, so I'm all right, but for years I've been in partnership with George Antoniou, the young fellow who works with me for Evans, and we have been forging antiquities."

"Well," said the policeman, "I don't know that that concerns me." "Yes," he said, "it does. Because we've sold a statuette of gold and ivory which was supposed to be a Cretan one to the Candia Government Museum, and that's a criminal offense. George is a scoundrel and I hate the fellow, and I've been waiting for this moment to give

A team of workers at Knossos in 1901.

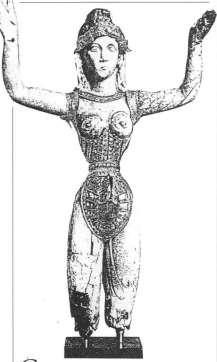

Chryselephantine statue of a goddess.

him away. Go straight to his house and you'll find all the forgeries and all our manufacturing plant there."

The police went, they raided, and they found exactly what he said, and they asked Evans to come and look, and I never saw so magnificent a collection of forgeries as those fellows had put together.

There were things in every stage of manufacture. For instance, people had been recently astounded at getting what they call chryselephantine statuettes from Crete; statuettes of ivory decked out with gold—there is one in the Boston Museum and one at Cambridge, and one in the Cretan Museum at Candia. These men were determined to do that sort of thing, and they had got there everything, from the plain ivory tusk and then the figure rudely carved out, then beautifully finished, then picked out with gold. And then the whole thing was put into acid, which ate away the soft parts of the ivory giving it the effect of having been buried for centuries. And I didn't see that anyone could tell the difference!

Sir Leonard Woolley
As I Seem to Remember,
1962

Cretan writing

The kingdom of Minos had mastered writing: From the eighteenth century BC on, the Minoans used clay tablets to inventory goods stored in the palace warehouses.

Evans was first drawn to Crete by his interest in finding writing from the Homeric period. His expectations were fulfilled when he discovered no fewer than three distinct forms of writing—excluding that used on the Phaistos disk, which remains undeciphered—hieroglyphics, Linear A, and Linear B. He believed that they represented three types of notation for the same language, that of the Minoan kings and palace administrators. Specialists greeted these discoveries with guarded enthusiasm. In 1902 Salomon Reinach warned against "instant Oedipuses, who will be materializing everywhere, claiming to have read tablets containing Finnish, Hebrew, Breton dialect, or even Homeric Greek." Evans worked out the numbering system and the meaning of certain ideograms but, absorbed as he was by the publication of his multivolume book *The Palace of Minos at Knossos,* he was unable to complete the deciphering task. We know today that only the hieroglyphics and Linear A served to write the language or languages of the Minoans, while Linear B was invented by the later Mycenaeans to transcribe their language, an early form of Greek. Linear B has been deciphered, but the earlier writing forms remain only partly understood.

Hieroglyphics and Linear A

Minoan hieroglyphics consist of 90 signs and an unknown number of ideograms. The only ideograms identified so far are those common to other forms of writing, such as those for *wine* and *figs.* Hieroglyphics were used in administrative documents of various kinds, and also had an ornamental

A seal-stone inscription with ornamental hieroglyphics.

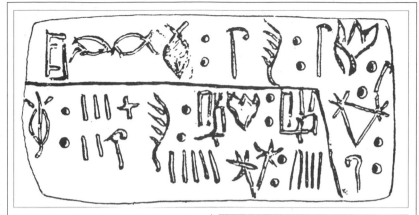

function on seal stones. Linear A is composed of 70 signs and at least 164 ideograms. It appears on tablets in "page" format, three- or four-sided clay bars, disks, stone or clay vases, and metal objects. The Minoans used hieroglyphics and Linear A simultaneously. Both were syllabic, but it is not clear whether they were used to write the same language or two different languages. None of these documents has yet been deciphered. We possess, in fact, fewer than two thousand examples of the hieroglyphics and fewer than ten thousand of Linear A. Thus, what Crete is awaiting is not a new master linguist, as Henri Berr thought in 1923, but rather discoveries of additional documents. When the British scholars Michael Ventris and John Chadwick deciphered Linear B in 1952 they had thirty thousand occurrences to study. By deduction and comparison, however, we can determine the subject matter of some documents. One hieroglyphic tablet (above) from Phaistos contains two irregular lines listing four products—wheat, grasses,

Minoan hieroglyphics (top) and Linear A (above) have yet to be deciphered, but it is known that these tablets deal with tax assessments and the distribution of goods.

olives, and figs—represented by ideograms and followed by a figure. In a document of the same type in Linear A [previous page, right column], discovered at Hagia Triada, the first line includes a word that must be a place name, whereas the second begins with the ideogram for wine. There follows a list of six words (probably anthroponyms) and numerals. The last line gives the sum of the quantities indicated on the preceding lines. Thus, this proves to be an archival document showing the distribution of exact quantities of wine in one region of the kingdom.

Linear B

Linear B is also a syllabic language, made up of eighty-seven syllabograms and about one hundred ideograms. Contrary to Evans's belief, it records a language that is a form of Greek. This writing is also found in the archives of mainland palaces of an earlier era—at Mycenae, Thebes, and Pylos, for instance. These documents are in the form of unfired clay tablets, either oblong (palm-leaf shape) or rectangular ("page" format). The tablets were not intended to be preserved; they were baked accidentally in the fires that destroyed the Minoan palaces. They were probably rough drafts in which officials of the kingdom made quick notes, perhaps to be copied later in more permanent materials that have not been found.

Fairly precise studies have been made of the work of these officials. One set of tablets (opposite), which Evans carefully removed from the palace of Knossos, proved to be a sort of "card file" that had fallen from its box during the conflagration that destroyed the palace; its seven tablets all deal with the same subject. On six tablets the administrator inventoried the quantities produced of each of the (unidentified) goods named; the bottom tablet summed up the data contained on the other six. According to handwriting analyses there were about one hundred officials writing such documents in the service of the Mycenaean rulers of Knossos. They also had helpers—children and elderly persons, to judge by fingerprints in the clay—who produced tablets on demand.

The function of writing in Crete

The documents inscribed in clay were primarily administrative records of commodities. Evans realized this well before any of the writing was deciphered. Thanks to the texts in Linear B, today we have a remarkably precise idea of the administrative organization of the kingdom at the time following the Mycenaean conquest. The accounts are mainly concerned with inventory and taxation: Palace officials calculated the portion of produce that was owed to the royal storehouses and kept track of what had been collected. These levies made it possible to build up reserves of foodstuffs and other merchandise that officials could draw upon for various purposes: food rations for slaves and artisans, offerings to the gods, military equipment for soldiers, and so forth. This is a valuable source of information for historians, even if it is limited by its narrowly specialized nature. For example, we know the names of certain Cretan bulls, but we do not have the name of a single king.

Alexandre Farnoux

Tablets with Linear B inscriptions, as discovered by Evans at Knossos.

Further Reading

GENERAL WORKS
ON ARTHUR EVANS

Brown, Ann, *Before Knossos: Arthur Evans' Travels in the Balkans and Crete*, 1995

Evans, Joan, *Time and Chance: The Story of Arthur Evans and His Forebears*, 1943

Horwitz, Sylvia L., *The Find of a Lifetime: Sir Arthur Evans and the Discovery of Knossos*, 1981

ON MINOAN CIVILIZATION
AND THE EXCAVATION
SITES

Branigan, Keith, *Pre-Palatial: The Foundations of Palatial Crete*, 1969, repr. 1988

Castleden, Rodney, *Minoans: Life in Bronze Age Crete*, 1990

Cotterell, Arthur, *The Minoan World*, 1979

Graham, James W., et al., *The Palaces of Crete*, 1987

Hood, Sinclair, *The Minoans: Crete in the Bronze Age*, 1971

Hutchinson, Richard W., *Prehistoric Crete*, 1962

Marinatos, Spiridon N., *Minoan Religion: Ritual, Image, and Symbol*, 1993

Platon, Nicolaos, *Crete*, 1968

——, *Zakros: The Discovery of a Lost Palace of Ancient Crete*, 1971

Willetts, R. F., *The Civilization of Ancient Crete*, repr. 1976

ON KNOSSOS

Castleden, Rodney, *The Knossos Labyrinth: A New View of the "Palace of Minos" at Knossos*, 1990

Cottrell, Leonard, *The Bull of Minos*, 1958

Hood, Sinclair, and Smyth, D., *Archaeological Survey of the Knossos Area*, British School at Athens, 1981

Michalidou, A., *Knossos*, 1987

CHAPTER I

Cornelius, *Creta Sacra*, 1755

Dontas, Domna N., *Greece and the Great Powers 1863–1875*, 1966

Elliadi, M. N., *Crete, Past and Present*, 1977

Hoeck, K., *Kreta*, 1823–29

Hopkins, Adam, *Crete: Its Past, Present and People*, 1977

Pashley, Robert, *Travels in Crete*, 1837

Pococke, Richard, *A Description of the East*, vol. 2, 1745

Spratt, Thomas A. B., *Travels and Researches in Crete*, 1865, repr. 1984

CHAPTER II

Deuel, Leo, *Memoirs of Heinrich Schliemann*, 1978

Falkener, E., *A Description of Some Important Theatres and Other Remains in Crete*, 1854

Milchhoefer, A., *Die Anfaenge der Kunst in Griechenland*, 1883

Perrot, Georges, and Chipiez, Charles, *History of Art in Primitive Greece*, trans. I. Gonino, 1894

Schliemann, Heinrich, *Mycenae*, 1878

——, "Schliemann's Letters to Max Müller in Oxford," *Journal of Hellenic Studies* 82 (1962): 75–105

CHAPTER III

Allsebrook, Mary, *Born to Rebel: The Life of Harriet Boyd Hawes*, 1992

Doorway of a house in Khania, from the Venetian period.

Brown, Ann C., *Arthur Evans and the Palace of Minos*, 1983

Driessen, Jan, *An Early Destruction in the Mycenaean Palace at Knossos*, 1990

Evans, Arthur J., "Excavations at Knossos," *Annual of the British School at Athens*, vols. 6, 11, 1900–1906

Oulié, Marthe, and de Saussure, Hermine, *La Croisière de La Perlette*, 1924

Pendlebury, John D. S., *The Archaeology of Crete: An Introduction*, 1939, repr. 1969

CHAPTER IV

Evans, Arthur J., *The Palace of Minos at Knossos*, 4 vols., 1921–36

Hood, Sinclair, and Taylor, William, *The Bronze Age Palace at Knossos: Plans and Sections*, British School at Athens, 1981

Pendlebury, John D. S., *A Handbook to the Palace of Minos, Knossos, with Its Dependencies*, 1933

Wunderlich, Hans G., *The Secret of Crete*, 1974

CHAPTER V

Bammer, Anton, "Wien und Kreta: Jugendstil und minoische Kunst,"

Jahreshefte des Oesterreichischen archäologischen Institutes in Wien 60 (1990): 130–51

Baurain, C., "Minos et la Thalassocratie Minoenne," *Aegeum* 7 (1991): 255–66

Burrows, Ronald M., *The Discoveries in Crete and Their Bearing on the History of Ancient Civilisation*, 1907

Clarke, T. H., "Prehistoric Sanitation in Crete," *British Medical Journal*, 1903

Deonna, Waldemar, *Les Toilettes Modernes de la Crète Minoenne*, 1911

Dussaud, René, *Les Civilisations Préhelléniques*, 2d ed., 1914

Glotz, Gustave, *The Aegean Civilisation*, 1925, repr. 1968

Hafner, German, *Art of Crete, Mycenae, and Greece*, 1968

Hawes, Charles H., and Boyd, Harriet, *Crete, the Forerunner of Greece*, 1909, repr. 1977

Higgins, Reynold, *Minoan and Mycenaean Art*, 1967

Stobart, John Clarke, *The Glory that Was Greece*, 1911

Chronology

Dates are approximate

3200 BC: Early Minoan period begins
2200 BC: Middle Minoan period begins
2000–1800 BC: Construction of the first palaces (Knossos, Phaistos, Mallia, and Zakro) (First Palace period)
1700 BC: Destruction of the first palaces
1650–1450 BC: Reconstruction of the palaces (Second Palace period)
1500 BC: Eruption of a volcano on Thera (Santorini); possible earthquake on Crete
1450 BC: Mycenaean invasion and destruction of the Minoan palaces
1370 BC: Final destruction of Knossos
1100–800 BC: Disappearance of Bronze Age civilizations on Crete and development of urban civilization
500 BC: Law Code of Gortyna
Late fourth century BC–first century AD (Hellenistic period) Ongoing rivalry among cities of Crete. Cretan piracy
67 BC: Roman conquest of Crete. Crete integrated into the Roman province of Cyrenaica, with Gortyna as capital
AD 324: Annexation of Crete by the Byzantine Empire
823: Arab conquest of Crete
961: Crete retaken by the Byzantines
1204: Venetian conquest of Byzantium during the Fourth Crusade; Crete ceded to the Venetians, seized briefly by Genoa
1221–1669: Venetian occupation; Cretan

renaissance, beginning in the fourteenth century, produces the painter El Greco and the writer Vincenzo Cornaros, author of the epic poem *Erotokritos*
1415: Arrival of the Florentine Cristoforo Buondelmonti in Crete
1669–1898: Turkish occupation of Crete
1817: Visit of the botanist F. W. Sieber
1821–30: Greek war of independence
1830–40: Crete ruled by the viceroy of Egypt
1866: Destruction of the monastery of Arcadi during an attempted revolution
1878: First excavations at Knossos, by Minos Kalokairinos
1886: The archaeologist Heinrich Schliemann visits Knossos
1894: Arthur Evans first visits Crete

1898: Cretan autonomy and arrival of Prince George of Greece as high commissioner
1900: Beginning of principal excavations in Crete, at Knossos and Phaistos
1913: Crete becomes part of Greece (Treaty of London)
1915: Discovery of the palace of Mallia by Joseph Hazzidakis; excavations interrupted by World War I
1923: In postwar agreement with Turkey, departure of the last Muslims, replaced by Greeks from Asia Minor
1941: During World War II, German invasion and devastation of the island
1944: Liberation of Crete by the Allied armies
1952: Linear B deciphered
1961: Discovery of the palace of Zakro

List of Illustrations

Index

Acknowledgments

The author wishes to thank the following persons for their comments and assistance in assembling these documents: In Oxford, R. Hood and S. Hood, former director of the British School at Athens, A. Brown, Keeper of the Ashmolean Museum; N. Momigliano and V. Fotou, directors of research; in Athens, J. Driessen, member, and K. Christophi, archivist, of the French School of Athens; in Paris, Professor Philippe Bruneau, University of Paris–Sorbonne, and A. Pasquier, curator of Greek and Roman antiquities at the Louvre; and in Berlin, Assistant Professor V. Stürmer, Humbold University. The publishers would like to thank Louisa Kalokairinos, director of the Heraklion Historical Museum; Anne Nesteroff, Caterina d'Agostino, and Carla Bertini of the Icona agency, and Éditions Colin et Gallimard. Maquette for Documents section: Dominique Guillaumin. Maps: Patrick Mérienne, Tina Thompson.

Photograph Credits

Archaeological Museum, Heraklion 108. Archaeological Museum, Tarquinia 116. Albert Kahn Archives, Boulogne 66a, 104b. Artephot/Held, Paris 95, Artephot/Nimatallah, Paris 88, 105, 110, Artephot/P. Trelay 84–85, Artephot/R. Percheron, Paris 61, 136b, Artephot/Takase, Paris 94, Artephot/P. Trelay, Paris, back cover. Ashmolean Museum, Oxford 30–31, 33c, 34, 40a, 40–41, 41, 42–43b, 43a (inset), 44, 46–47, 49, 50b, 51l, 51r, 63, 76c, 76–77, 78–79, 80–81, 82–83, 84a, 86r, 86–87, 89, 90–91, 92–93a, 92–93b, 145a, 159. Bibliothèque Nationale, Paris 12, 13, 14–15b, 56–57, 64b, 103a, 103b, 114. Blake and Mortimer, based on E. P. Jacobs, Brussels 124. Bridgeman Art Library, London 109b. British Museum, London 14–15a. Cinémathèque Française, Paris 125. Arthur Evans, *The Palace of Minos at Knossos,* 17, 18, 19, 23, 38br, 38–39a, 38–39b, 42–43a, 60, 62–63, 64–65, 66b, 67, 68–69, 70l, 70b, 70–71, 71b, 72, 73b, 74, 74–75, 75a, 76b, 77b, 82–83, 85, 86l, 96–97, 98, 98–99, 99, 102a, 104a, 106a, 106b, 107, 109a, 118, 120–21, 122, 126, 127a, 127b, 129, 132–33, 143, 145b, 146, 147, 149. Dagli-Orti, Paris 4c, 5c, 7, 9c, 25, 28–29, 35, 45, 64a, 73l, 102b, 134, 135, 137, 138, 139. Edition Errance/Colin, Paris 128, 130, 131. Editions Millet, Paris 100–101b, Editions Millet/C. Ferrare 32, 33a, 50a, 51b, 112; Editions Millet/F. Brosse 2–3, 4–5a, 4–5b, 6, 8–9a, 8–9b. Explorer/D. Clement, Paris 124, Explorer/Hervé Negre, Paris 114–15, Explorer/H. Veiller, Paris, spine. French School of Athens 30, 52–53, 143. Gallimard Jeunesse/E. Tweedy 36a, 36b, 37a, 37b, Gallimard Jeunesse/P. Horvais 38ar. Gennadius Library, Athens 16–17. Gerola family, Istituto Veneto di Scienze, Lettere ed Arti, Venice 26, 54–55, 58–59, 150. Italian School of Athens 24–25. N. Kontos and N. Dessylas, Greece 20b, 20–21c, 21b. Erich Lessing/Art Resource, New York, front cover. Magnum/E. Lessing, Paris 8c, 24 (inset), 111. Musée du Louvre, Department of Greek Antiquities/C. Larrieu, Paris 31. National Geographic Society/Lloyd K. Townsend, Washington, D.C. 140–41. National Museum, Athens 28, 29, 62. Pinacothèque Nationale, Athens 20–21a. With the kind permission of Oxbow Books, Oxford 53. Royal Ontario Museum, Toronto 76a. Sirot-Angel, Paris 48–49. Staatliche Museen Preussischer Kulturbesitz/Isolde Luckert, Berlin 27. Vatican Library, Rome 22. Vatican Museums, Rome 117.

Text Credits

Grateful acknowledgment is made for use of material from the following: pp. 28–29: Richmond Lattimore, *The Odyssey of Homer,* New York: Harper & Row, 1965, 1967 © Richmond Lattimore, 1965, 1967, copyright renewed. Reprinted by permission of HarperCollins Publishers, Inc.; pp. 74, 88: Arthur Evans, *The Palace of Minos at Knossos,* London: Macmillan, 1921, vols. I, 3; p. 75: Richmond Lattimore, *The Iliad of Homer,* Chicago: University of Chicago Press, 1951; p. 113: Mary Renault, *The King Must Die,* © 1958 by Mary Renault, Pantheon Books (New York); pp. 118–19, 122–23: Robert Graves, *The Greek Myths,* vol. I, Baltimore: Penguin, 1955; pp. 119–22: Roberto Calasso, *The Marriage of Cadmus and Harmony,* New York: Knopf, 1993; pp. 128–31: Micheline Van Effenterre and Michel Mastorakis, *Les Minoens: L'Âge d'Or de Crète,* Paris: Errance, 1991; pp. 140–43: Hugh Sackett and Sandy MacGillivray, "Boyhood of a God," *Archaeology* 42, no. 5 (September–October 1989): 26–31 (Copyright the Archaeological Institute of America, 1989, reproduced by permission of *Archaeology Magazine*); pp. 144–45: Sir Leonard Woolley, *As I Seem to Remember,* London: Allen and Unwin on behalf of Shaftsbury and District Society and Museum Society, 1962.

Sir Arthur Evans at Knossos, c. 1920 (opposite).

Alexandre Farnoux studied at the Ecole
Française d'Athènes (the French School of Athens).
He teaches Greek history at the University of Strasbourg,
France, and conducts research in Crete on the Minoan
civilization. He is director of the excavation of a
residential quarter in the Minoan city of Mallia.

Translated from the French by David J. Baker

For Harry N. Abrams, Inc.
Editors: Eve Sinaiko, Richard Wilkinson
Typographic Designer: Elissa Ichiyasu
Design Supervisor: Miko McGinty
Assistant Designer: Tina Thompson
Text Permissions: Barbara Lyons

Library of Congress Catalog Card Number: 96–83347

ISBN 0–8109–2819–1